BOHERNABREENA

GW00670462

PETER QUINN

The
History
Press
Ireland

First published 2015

The History Press Ireland
50 City Quay
Dublin 2
Ireland
www.thehistorypress.ie

British Library Cataloguing in Publication Data.
A catalogue record for this book is available from the British Library.

ISBN 978 1 84588 887 9

Typesetting and origination by The History Press

Printed and bound in Great Britain by TJ International Ltd, Padstow

CONTENTS

ACKNOWLEDGEMENTS

My thanks to South County Dublin Library who allowed me to use photographs from the Michael Fewer Collection, Charles Russell Collection, Patrick Healy Collection and The Tallaght Historical Society Collection.

INTRODUCTION

I grew up in Bohernabreena, never realising the extent to which I was surrounded by ancient history. There was little remaining of the ancient world, except for one obvious exception: the still-standing shell of the Hellfire Club. As children we would often be told by the older folk of the goings-on in that notorious place; they seemed to take great delight in relaying the tale of the 'Devil' himself playing cards there.

Ruins that I saw as a child were remnants of a rich history, long forgotten. The only time I remember hearing a reference to the valley's glorious past was on a school trip; passing a wooded area at the back of Glenasmole we were told that Fionn McCumhaill had trained the Fianna in the area. They perfected the art of running through the forest without so much as breaking a stick underfoot. This allowed them to steal up on deer or enemies without making a sound – the Irish version of ninja warriors. It was many years later when I was reading a book of Irish legends to my own children that I came across the story of Tír na nÓg

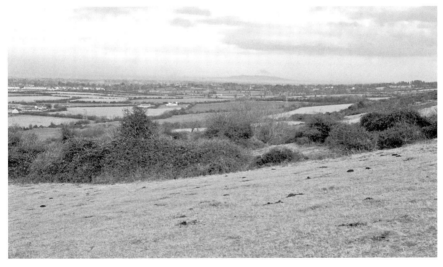

A fine example of a ring fort at Bohernabreena. It is 30 yards in diameter. (Courtesy of South County Dublin Library)

and as Oisín fell from his horse, there on the page right in front of me it gave the location as 'The Valley of Thrushes' (Glenasmole). My interest was aroused enough for me to start digging and I slowly uncovered one story after another. During my search, I found fragments here and pieces there, and some extensive works on the area. I decided to put everything together that was of interest, from the earliest stories to the present day, and write them up in a way that was easier to read than the older writing I used as resources. I wanted to bring the stories to life again, the way they had come to life for me – and that is how this book came to be.

There is evidence of settlements and communities that lived and worked in the Glenasmole Valley going back 5,000 years. The oldest and finest example is the megalithic burial chamber on Seefin Mountain, complete with engravings in the stone. There have been archaeological finds in the area representing all the major eras: the Stone Age, Iron Age and Bronze Age.

It is thought that up until about AD 400 the druid community in the area buried their dead at (what is now known as) St Anne's burial ground, which overlooks the reservoir. This druid burial place became St Sanctan's 1,500 years ago. Sanctan built the first church in the valley (of which there are remains). He was the son of a Cornish king who was a descendant of the famous 'Old King Cole'.

There is land in the valley (where the church of Sanctan was built) that was owned by the Priory of St John of Jerusalem, a division of the legendary Knights Templar, in the fourteenth century. I spent some time at the site looking at the stones in the ruin to see if there were any markings in them that might suggest a deeper connection with the Templars, like Roslyn chapel in Scotland. I didn't find any.

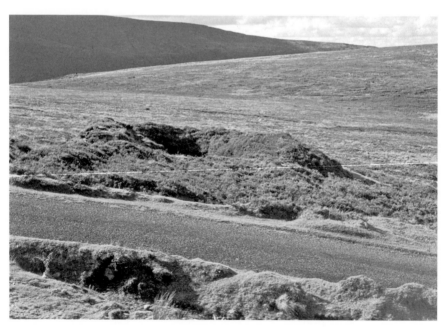

An ice house at Glenasmole, used to store ice which was later sold in the city. (Courtesy of South County Dublin Library)

The list of characters, saints, hell raisers and legends who lived in or frequented the area of Bohernabreena and Glenasmole over the years is quite impressive. The first story recounts a battle over 2,000 years ago and is one of the oldest known complete Irish sagas: 'The Destruction of Dá Derga's Hostel'. The route to the hostel gave Bohernabreena its name, 'The Road to the Court', and inspired James Joyce's story 'The Dead' (the last story in his book *Dubliners*). The actual translation of the word '*breen*' is vague: it has been described by some as a mansion, and by others as a hostel, a great hall or court. Dá Derga's Hostel as described in the story had forty rooms, so by anyone's standards it would have been a mansion. These *breens* were used by all, from the humble traveller to the High King's of Ireland as they made their way across the country.

The infamous Hellfire Club held their decadent parties on the top of Montpelier Hill in the hunting lodge that is named after the sacrilegious meetings that were held there. The original name of the hill has long been forgotten.

The rebellious character of Buck Whaley, the head of the Irish branch of the Hellfire Club, was probably the most notorious and decadent hell raiser the valley has ever seen, not to mention Dublin city. The club's ideals, their hatred of the Church and the stories that are still told of what happened there lend a sinister but intriguing aspect to the area's history.

I am not a historian but I have searched and researched over a number of years to make this work as accurate and complete as I possibly could.

1

PREHISTORY

The valley's remarkable landscape was shaped by thawing glaciers during the Ice Age. The ice sheets from the midlands plastered lime-rich sand along the sides of the valley walls and pushed right up to the centre until, depleted by climatic change, it halted, leaving in its wake a great moraine which was used by the dam builders in the 1880s to impound the river (the reservoir). The post-glacial valley floor was U-shaped and much higher than at present but the Dodder and its tributaries cut through the sand, especially at the western end of the glen to cut deeper into the valley floor.

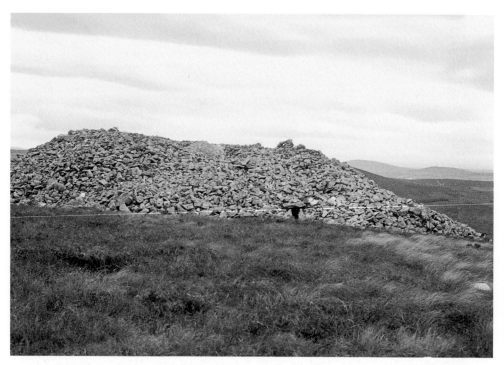

The 5,000-year-old passage tomb at Seefin, one of the finest in the Dublin/Wicklow hills. (Courtesy of South County Dublin Library)

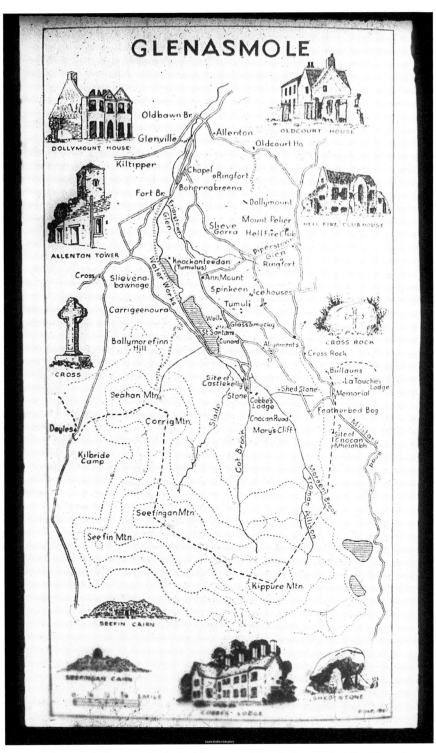

Map of Glenasmole by Patrick Healy. (Courtesy of South County Dublin Library)

The valley is rich in prehistoric landmarks with burial cairns on the hilltops and a megalithic passage tomb. These ancient tombs, together with the stone circles and ring forts in the area are all visible today and are a reminder of the people that once lived in the valley. The stories of the Fianna, who favoured Glenasmole as their hunting ground, and the earlier story of Dá Derga's Hostel give a small idea of the life and aspirations of the people who lived all those centuries ago. It also shows that Glenasmole was throughout history a celebrated place.

THE SHED STONE

The Shed Stone is said to mark the position of a buried treasure. Although this has the general appearance of a prehistoric dolmen or portal tomb, it is obvious on close examination that the supporting stones are actually three pieces of one stone which must have been split by the weight of the larger one above. These three fragments are not placed to form a chamber or enclosure, which would be one of the chief characteristics of a prehistoric burial place. It would appear therefore that the unusual arrangement of these stones is purely coincidental. The height is about 4ft.

SEEFIN

The most interesting monument in the area must be the narrow and elaborately decorated passage leading into the burial chamber on Seefin (The Seat of Finn). One of the projecting stones near the entrance has a faint etching, although the design is hard to make out. Two of the massive upright supports on the right-hand side of the passage are said to have shallow spiral engravings. The huge cairn on

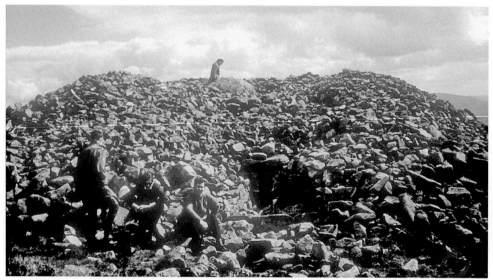

In this picture of the passage tomb at Seefin it is possible to make out where the roof collapsed in the centre. (Courtesy of South County Dublin Library)

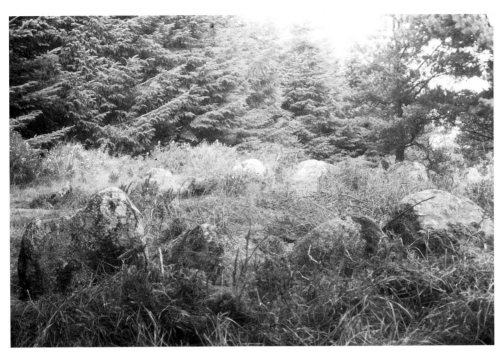

The stone circle at Ballinascorney. (Courtesy of South County Dublin Library)

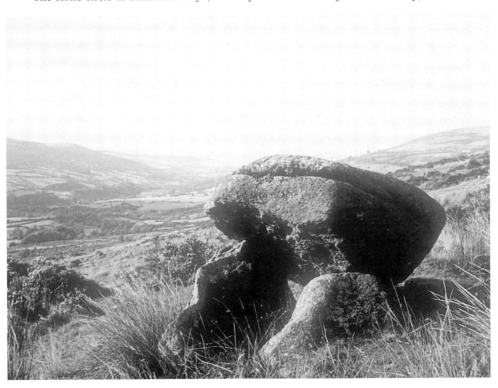

The Shed Stone. (Courtesy of South County Dublin Library)

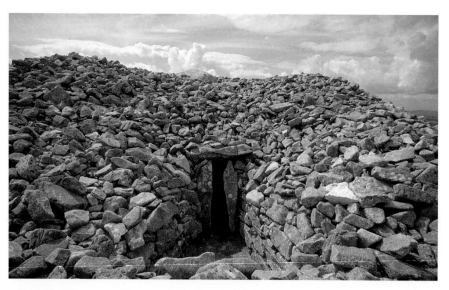

The Seefin passage tomb. (Rob Hurson, Wikimedia Commons)

top – a full 24m across and 3m high – is already quite impressive, but as you circle around to the north, the exposed entrance, with its massive lintel and posts, gives the first real taste of what lies within. From here, a 7m long passage extends back into the corbelled central chamber, now open to the sky since the capstones were removed.

In 1931 a party of archaeologists led by Professor Macalister cleared out the loose stones and revealed the original entrance passage, 7m long and very low and narrow. There were two recesses on each side of the chamber and one at the end. No finds were made during the work.

SEAHAN

There are no less than three megalithic tombs on Seahan. Two are large cairns. The cairn to the east is a passage tomb, over 21m in diameter, with a kerb of elongated granite stones. On top of the cairn a capstone sits over the central chamber.

The second cairn, now topped with a trig pillar, is almost 24m in diameter and 2m high. It appears never to have been opened. A short distance further west lie the shattered remains of a wedge tomb – a kind of burial that is considered unusual above 300m.

Both of these monuments were built on the stony surface of the mountain top, apparently before the growth of peat which now covers the mountain. On the Down Survey map of 1655 and on Rocque's map of 1760 this mountain is named 'Seavick na Bantree' or 'the seat of the widow's son' and maps of the early part of the last century call it 'Slieve Baun' or 'the white mountain'.

From this mountain the county boundary runs westward until it crosses the road near Kilbride Camp. Just at this point and on the Dublin side of the boundary is Doyle's farmhouse, which is the highest dwelling house in Ireland, at 428m above sea level.

ARCHAEOLOGICAL FINDS AT PIPERSTOWN

Piperstown is said to be named after a piper who sat on the granite stone (which is still in place) and played his pipes for locals. His name was Cornan and he lived in a small village on the lower side of the road. As time went on, people often referred to the village as Piperstown.

In the 1950s a gorse fire on the southern slopes of Piperstown Mountain revealed the presence of a total of fifteen prehistoric sites, eight of which appear to be burial cairns and the remainder habitation or hut sites and cooking sites which were dated to Neolithic (new Stone Age) and Bronze Age (2,000 BC–400 BC). In the 1980s a mechanical digger removing sand overlay from a quarry site uncovered a Bronze Age burial cist at Piperstown lower down the valley.

An enormous quantity of struck flints, over 600, found within an enclosure, clearly demonstrated that intensive flint working was carried on at this site and the disposal of these flakes shows that the work was done under cover. Such a concentration of flake artefacts (which may be part of an arrow or javelin head) would suggest that the flint worker was providing not only for his own needs but also for those of a community.

Piperstown differs from all other sites in the area in that it comprises both habitation sites and burial places of people who probably belonged to one community and one period. In this it is almost unique among Irish prehistoric sites.

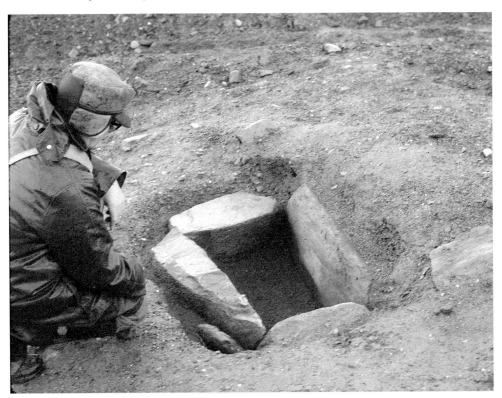

Cist at Piperstown. (Courtesy of South County Dublin Library)

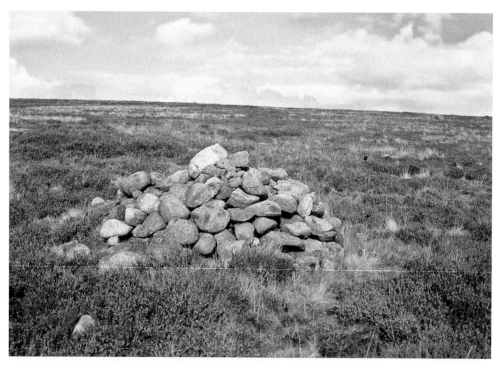

A cairn at Piperstown. (Courtesy of South County Dublin Library)

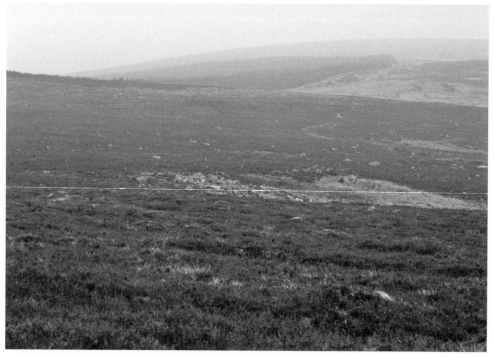

Piperstown group of huts and cairns. (Courtesy of South County Dublin Library)

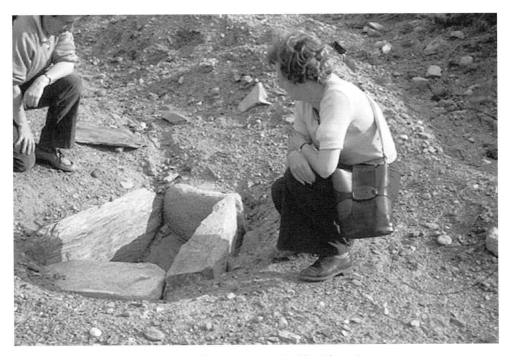

The Piperstown dig. (Courtesy of South County Dublin Library)

What must surely be the most valuable object ever found in the Glenasmole Valley was reported in the Dublin papers of 1788:

> Last week as some labourers belonging to Mr. O'Dogherty of Glenasmole were cutting turf, one of them discovered a gold crown at about four inches deep. It is about seven inches in diameter and weighs eleven ounces. It is perhaps the crown of some provincial king before the introduction of Christianity. There are several figures raised on it but no such thing as a cross.

The crown is not in the possession of the museum as most of the artefacts found at this time or earlier were taken out of the country, or sold on.

There is at present in the National Museum a weaver's comb made of horn which was found in Glassamucky bog. It is the only one of its type ever found in Ireland and is believed to be of Iron Age date.

Archaeology gives us a good idea of the people who lived here. It takes us back to the development of farming in Neolithic times, when organised communities cultivated the lowland fringes of the central plain, yet buried their eminent dead in elaborate hilltop tombs. The similarities in construction and symbolism all point to a common social and religious outlook. As far as the hills themselves are concerned, even at that early stage, the human impact on the terrain was already quite notable. From an examination of the pollen record preserved deep in the bog (and one such study was made precisely in the area between Seefin and Seefingan), there is evidence of the prehistoric clearance of trees for pasture and of the later burning of the land that replaced the woods.

In Glenasmole, where different quality of land prevailed, over relatively small spaces a very clever management system was utilised to maximise the potential yield from the land in the area. The system has been compared to the pattern typical of Highland Scotland known as 'rundale', which integrates arable, meadow, grazing and bogland into a production system managed communally. It is seen as an egalitarian system that gave everyone living in the cluster a share of the different land types, though not an equal share. So in the glen below farmers would have arable plots, meadowland, grazing rights and the right to cut turf (turbary) on

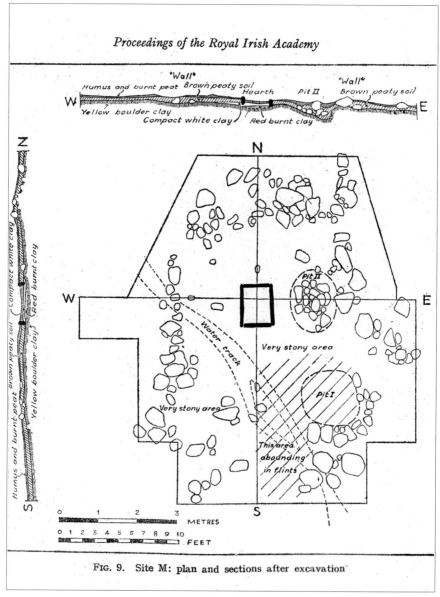

FIG. 9. Site M: plan and sections after excavation

A map of the dig at Piperstown. (Courtesy of South County Dublin Library)

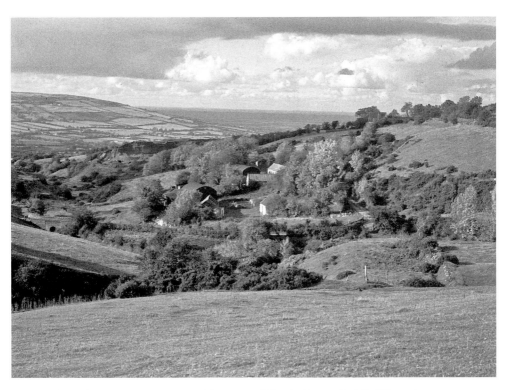

Looking down onto Piperstown. (Courtesy of South County Dublin Library)

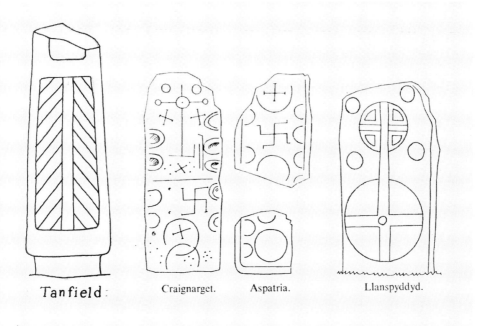

Tanfield. Craignarget. Aspatria. Llanspyddyd.

Stone grave illustrations. (Courtesy of South County Dublin Library)

the bogland. Such a system implied that the landscape in general was unenclosed. The grazing rights on the mountain were allocated by a complicated procedure in which the livestock unit was known as a collop and each farmer's stock, especially sheep, had to have an identifying mark. The only functioning elements of rundale operating today are the grazing and turbary rights and the landscape below is now enclosed in small fields. But if it were possible to examine in detail the ownership of these we would find a fragmented pattern which could be traced back to rundale.

Although the house clusters in Glenasmole have the characteristic siting pattern of clusters, in general they were built by the landlord (Cobbe) in the 1840s and his management system was very successful, both to landlord and tenant.

In the valley, the evidence that has been found of Ireland's oldest settlements, forms and origins has been the subject of much debate.

2

HIGH KING CONAIRE MÓR AND DÁ DERGA'S HOSTEL

In Pre-Christian Ireland kings were held in the highest esteem. They were believed to be responsible for the weather, the crops and the health of the livestock, and they had to appear to live up to these supernatural standards in their daily life. The King of Tara was like any other leader affected by this public expectation and had many constraints or '*gesas*' to abide by. These were personalised rules that were given to each new king. To break one of these rules meant certain disaster for the king. Even a blemish on his skin could mean the end of his reign as it would have been seen as a terrible omen, a sign that the king was not immune to human frailty.

Conaire Mór's mother was the daughter of Cormac, King of Ulster, and Etain. (There are other source notes that differ.) The king wanted a son but Etain gave birth to a daughter. Cormac ordered the newborn to be thrown in a pit to die. The king's orders were being carried out when the child smiled and softened the hearts of the two men who could not now leave her in the pit. Instead, she was taken in by a cowherd and christened Mesbuachalla (meaning the cowherd's foster child). She was kept hidden from Cormac in a house with only a roof opening and a window for fear that she might be seen. One day, so the legend goes, she was visited by a bird that flew in through the roof opening. The bird landed beside her and the feathers fell away from it as it grew larger and finally, when all the feathers had fallen to the floor, the bird had become a young man (depicted in drawings as an Adonis) and the story discreetly tells us that she gave her love to the young man who was a god. Before leaving he told her that she would bear a son whose name would be Conary and he would be forbidden to hunt birds (this was one of Conaire Mór's *gesas*) and would be the High King of Ireland.

De Shíl Chonairi Móir (On the Descendants of Conaire Mór) tells the story of how Conaire became King of Tara. It was a peaceful era and all was well. There are three records of his kingship that all date him before Christ but the exact dates vary by about 100 years from one source to another. Why have I written about a King of Tara? Well, according to a story called 'Togail Bruidne Dá Derga' (The Destruction of Dá Derga's Hostel), he met his untimely death at a hostel that was built at the back of the Glenasmole Valley.

> Tis by him [Dá Derga] that the Hostel was built, and since it was built its doors have never been shut save on the side to which the wind comes — the valve is closed against it — and since he began housekeeping his caldron was never taken from the fire, but it has been boiling food for the men of Erin.
>
> An excerpt from 'Togail Bruidne Dá Derga' translated by Whitley Stokes, DCL

The Destruction of Dá Derga's Hostel is recounted in the *Book of Lecan* and the *Book of Dun Cow*. As well as being the oldest Irish saga, it is among the few complete narratives of any great extent preserved from ancient Irish literature. The translation from Irish to English was the work of Dr Whitley Stokes (published as *Togail Bruidne Dá Derga* (The Destruction of Dá Derga's Hostel) in 1910) constructed by him from eight manuscripts, the oldest going back to about AD 1100. The saga existed in written form as early as the eighth or ninth century. The following extract is taken from the book's introduction:

> One of the epic Irish tales, The Destruction of Dá Derga's Hostel is a specimen of remarkable beauty and power. The primitive aspects of the story are made evident in the way that the plot turns upon the disasters that follow on the violation of taboos (the gesas) by the monstrous nature of many of the warriors, and by the absence of any attempt to explain the beliefs implied or the marvels related in it.

The name Bohernabreena in its original Irish form, *Bothar-na-Bruighne*, is one of the ancient Irish place names. Translated it means the 'road to the court', or 'great mansion'. The house of Dá Derga was one of six royal palaces or *breens*, houses of universal hospitality. These *breens* were situated on the five great roads from Tara in the Iron Age (400 BC–AD 400) there where the hospitality of chieftains was extended to all as they made their way across the country. One of these roads, known today as the Clonee Road, led from Tara, through Lucan, to Bohernabreena.

Dá Derga's Hostel, like all *breens*, was built on high ground, where it would afford an uncompromised view of the surrounding countryside. A hill mentioned in *Agallamh na Senorach* (Tales of the Elders) where a *bruidhean* was to be erected was called *Cnoc an Eolais* (Hill of Guidance) as a great fire was lit each night to illuminate the valleys below. This was common practice at all the *breens*. In the case of Dá Derga's Hostel it would have not only illuminated Glenasmole and Glencree but wider stretches of Dublin and Meath on one side and a large part of the Southern Cuala on the other. In the story, the raiders who attacked the hostel could see the fire when they were out at sea. It served as a beacon and was indispensable at a time when there were few roads and dense forestry in the lowlands.

Wherever a *breen* was erected the word breen was incorporated in the place name and so it is easy to identify the sites now. There were six chief hostels of Erin:

1. Bohernabreena in Dublin.
2. Mullaghnabreena near Ballysodare and Mullanabreena in Achonry both in Sligo. (It is thought that one of these hostels in Sligo must have been a chief hostel and the other a secondary hostel.)
3. Mullanabreen in County Tyrone.
4. Carrickbreeny in County Donegal.
5. Letterbreen in County Fermanagh.
6. Breenmore Hill in County Westmeath (near Athlone where there are remains of an old fort).

All of these *breens* were built on hills and hilltops with the exception of the last; Breenmore (the site of Bruidhean Da Coca), was on ground less than 500ft above sea level, but as the surrounding land is flat the illuminated house on the summit would have been seen for miles.

TOGAIL BRUIDNE DÁ DERGA (THE DESTRUCTION OF DÁ DERGA'S HOSTEL)

Now that we know what a *breen* was and why they were built, it's time to give you an overview of the story of The Destruction of Dá Derga's Hostel. The actual story is quite long so this is just a synopsis; if it wets your literary appetite I highly recommend you pick up a copy of the full tale.

Conaire Mór's reign was a peaceful and prosperous time for Ireland. The weather and harvests were good, there were fleets of foreign ships at the ports, 'no one slew another in Erin during his reign, and to everyone in Erin his fellow's voice seemed as sweet as the strings of lutes. From mid spring to mid autumn no wind disturbed a cow's tail.'

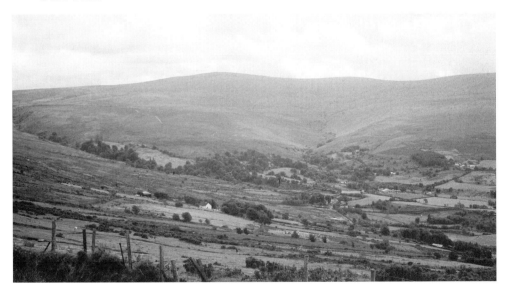

Looking at Kippure Mountain from Glenasmole Valley. (Courtesy of South County Dublin Library)

Conaire had made enemies, though. He had come down heavy on raiding (mostly stealing cattle) and quickly stamped it out throughout the country. Unfortunately his three foster brothers (grandsons of Donn Desa) were career raiders and when they were caught the people wanted them condemned to death but Conaire spared their lives and exiled them. The banished men left the country and on the seas they met another exiled chief, Ingcel the One-Eyed, son of the King of Britain and they banded together.

Knowing nothing but plundering, they returned to their old ways. Their first attack was on a fortress in which Ingcel's father, mother and brothers were guests of a local king and all were killed that night. Conaire's foster brothers were taken aback by the savagery of the attack and even more so when Ingcel announced they would raid Ireland next. It was decided they should increase their number (taking in mostly outlawed men) for the attack on Ireland. They travelled across the sea and took land on the Dublin coast near Howth. Nine men were chosen to climb to the summit at Howth and from the vantage point there they saw King Conaire Mór's cavalcade of more than one hundred chariots heading south on the Slighe Cualann.

Conaire Mór was returning from Thomond after settling a dispute and found he was cut off from Tara as the county was blazing with flame and dense smoke. (The historic fact behind this is the invasion by the Laginian tribes.) He and his party made for Dublin and the hills of Bohernabreena (the road to the court, the court being the hostel of Dá Derga) and Glenasmole.

As they approached they saw three men ahead of them, dressed entirely in red and riding red horses (the story begins to take a wonderful supernatural turn here as these men claim to be dead kings), but no matter how fast they rode behind they could not catch up.

One of Conaire Mór's *gesas* was that he could not leave Tara after sunset and could not stay away from Tara for more than nine days. He was also not to follow three red men to the red man's house (which he has just done and realises it in the story, when he arrives at the hostel). The story starts to give the reader or listener a feeling that there is a net slowly drawing tighter around Conaire.

Ingcel and his marauders got back into their ships and followed along the coast until the king's party reached Dá Derga's Hostel, and a large bonfire was lit that could be seen from the sea. Anyone who has walked to the top of Kippure will know the view over the sea is extensive and incorporates Leamore Strand.

While Conaire and his men settled into the hostel, an army of 5,000 men under Ingcel landed at either Merrion Strand or Leamore Strand near Greystones (both locations are disputed) and began to make their way to the hostel. The noise of the 150 boats carrying the 5,000 men running aground on the stony beach was heard and felt in the hostel and caused spears to fall from their places on the wall. (Because of the route the raiders took and the reference to the stony beach, Leamore is the more likely location for their landing.)

Ingcel instructed everyone to take a stone from the beach and carry it up through Glencree to Two Rock where the stones were piled (there is a stone cairn at the top). After the battle each man took a stone away and the remaining stones represented those lost in battle.

The descriptions of Conaire's men and of the hostel are detailed and give a great picture of the scene. Ingcel and his guides watched from nearby and, looking through the wheels of the chariots that formed a barrier around the hostel, they were able to observe everything by the light of the hostel bonfire. The hostel doors were all open (it is mentioned there were seven doors and they only closed the doors against the prevailing wind). The text describes in detail the many rooms in the hostel, accommodating people with various skills such as harpists and the best pipe-players in the whole world from the fairy hills of Bregia (County Meath). These are listed by name as Bind, Robind, Riarbind, Sihe, Dibe, Deicrind, Umal, Cumal and Ciallglind. There were also jugglers, king's aids, warriors, soldiers and waiters.

Ingcel, the grandsons of Donn Desa and their army surrounded the hostel and then attacked. During the battle, the raiders damned the river Dodder, which ran under the hostel, and then set the hostel on fire. With no water to put the fire out, the defenders resorted to using wine and what water they had to hold back the flame. Three times it was set alight and three times it was put out. Conaire asked for a drink as he was literally dying of thirst and his warrior Mac Cecht was sent off with Conaire's golden cup. He burst through the enemy surrounding the hostel and went to find water.

Mac Cecht's quest took him all across Ireland as the fairy folk, who control nature, had manifested their powers against Conaire because he had broken his *gesa*, and the lakes and wells all hid as Mac Cecht approached but one lake, Loch Gara in Roscommon, failed to hide itself in time and it was here he filled the golden cup.

When he arrived back the next morning, the battle was more or less over and Mac Cecht found Conaire dead and two of the raiders cutting off his head. Mac Cecht decapitated one and hurled a huge stone pillar at the other who was running off with Conaire's head. He fell dead to the ground. Mac Cecht picked up his master's head and poured the water into Conaire's mouth. Then the head spoke and thanked Mac Cecht for what he had done. The High King Conaire Mór died at Dá Derga's Hostel on All Souls' Day.

THE LOCATION OF DÁ DERGA'S HOSTEL

There have been many suggestions as to the site of the hostel, even Donnybrook was considered at one time but later ruled out as the artefacts recovered from the site were from a later period. Despite all the debate over the years, the exact location of Dá Derga's Hostel has never been proven. There are some commentators who believe it didn't exist at all. Henry Morris, in a paper published in October 1935, locates the site of Dá Derga's Hostel as being near the summit of Kippure, built over one of the three main brooks that feed the Dodder known as Moreen's brook, which is on the east of Kippure at the head of the Glenasmole Valley looking out to sea. Moreen's brook is, he states, simply an eclipsed form of Bruidhean following a preposition and the article, i.e. *ag an mBruidhin*. To back up his case Henry Morris included an ancient poem in his paper which described the route the raiders took from the east coast to the hostel, crossing both the top of the Sugarloaf and the Two Rock Mountain.

The poem is long so only the verses that apply to the journey are reproduced overleaf. As you can see, the mountains are named in Old Irish but Henry Morris in his paper translated and identified most of the places.

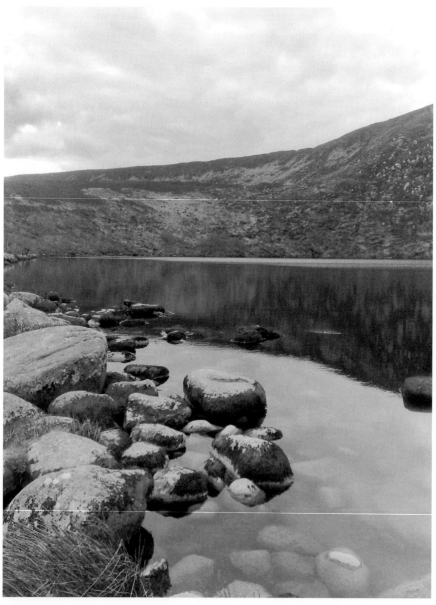

Lough Bray nestled in the shoulder of Kippure Mountain close to the proposed site of the hostel.

It was on the very night of Samain,
an occasion for foray and fighting,
up to Derg's oaken house, full of doors,
when they over-mastered Conaire.

This was their road from Long Laga [Leamore Strand],
along shallow Tond Uairbeoil [a tidal wave that comes in on the Wicklow coast].
to Glenn da Gruad across Gabar [the Glen of the Killincarrig River and
the Newcastle-Kilcoole-Windgate road]
across Suan [not identified] and across Senchora [not identified].

To the point of outlook clear
at Oe Cualann under like rule [Big Sugar Loaf],
to dark Cuilend [the Glencullen River], over Crecca [the Scalp],
over Sruthar [a stream draining from Two Rock going out to sea], over Sliab
Lecga [Two Rock Mountain].

The 'Mountain of Sobail' son of old Sengand,
by every certain lawful division,
till the time of Ingcel noble and splendid
was the original name of the ancient mountain.

The fact that the Dodder (which looks like a passive river but after heavy rainfall becomes a torrent) would have swept away a fort that was placed anywhere below the brooks that feed it (many bridges have been swept away by the force of the Dodder over the years) gives credence to Morris' argument for the location of Dá Derga's Hostel on the side of the Kippure Mountain, where the RTÉ mast now stands. It just so happens this is the highest point in Dublin and it gives a fantastic vantage point over the entire area. It is known as the 'roof of Dublin'.

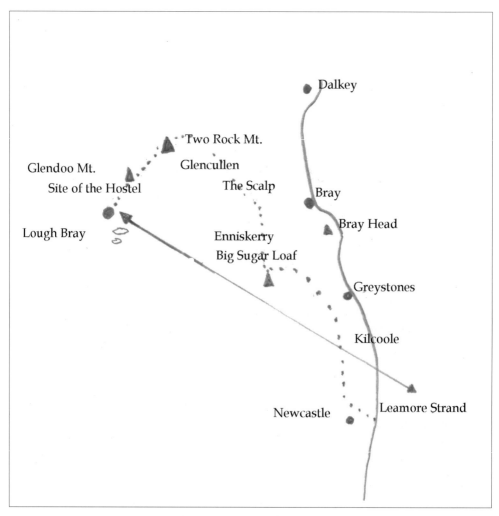

Map of the route the raiders took as described in the poem 'Ben Etair'. (Courtesy of South County Dublin Library)

3

FIONN MAC CUMHAILL AND THE FIANNA

Hereabouts – from Seskin to Seefin,
From Seechon to Ballamallick,
here it was that Fionn and Oscur slipped Bran,
Sceolan and Lomhair to course the red deer in a
chase which will reach no kill while poetry
is our heritage and Ireland our land.

From *Malachi Horan Remembers Rathfarnham and
Tallaght in the Nineteenth Century* (Mercier, 1943)

Almost every period of Ireland's settlement history is represented in the Glenasmole (Valley of the Thrushes). The old Irish poems relating to the glen describe it as one of the hunting grounds of the great warrior and statesman 'Finn Mac Coole' (Fionn Mac Cumhaill). Here, with the Fianna, he chased the enchanted doe with his great hounds, Bran and Sgeolan. The old poems relate to events occurring in the very earliest times, and, like all such legends, are partly fiction and partly fact. The glen must have been a much-celebrated spot at the time. It was probably wooded up to the tops of the hills which surround it, for many traces of trees remain in the bogs which now cover the sides of Kippure, Seefin, Carrigeen, and the other hills around. In these wild woods it is said Fionn trained his men, perfecting the art of running through the forestry without breaking the sticks underfoot, so they could silently close in on an enemy or hunt the red deer that roamed the valley.

The legends of the adventures of Fionn Mac Cumhaill and the Fianna have a timeless appeal. The story of the Salmon of Knowledge or Tír na nÓg (considered to be the finest in the collection) is a story that, once heard, stays with you. These stories were told for centuries, so by the time they were written down they were well honed and formed, and as a result wonderfully memorable with plenty of supernatural events and heroic feats to keep the listeners' attention.

The best sources of these stories remain the translations by the Ossianiac Society, who, realising the value of the tales, translated them faithfully to preserve them

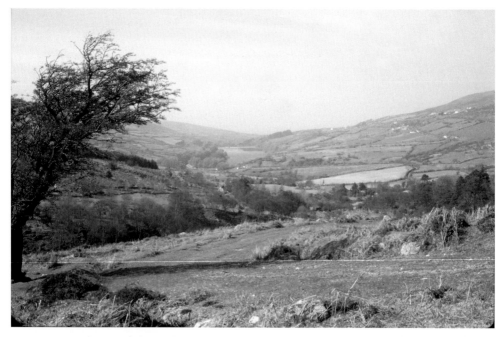

The picturesque valley of Glenasmole, the Fianna's favourite hunting ground. (Courtesy of South County Dublin Library)

for future generations. This was during the Celtic revival and the members of the society were educated Irish writers. Lady Gregory also published translations for which Yeats wrote an introduction; they are still available today. In these tales fantastic, supernatural events happen without explanation but really add to that epic sense of the story. Take for example 'The Chase of Glenasmole' – for no apparent reason but to increase tension and become larger than life, a battle which begins with ordinary warriors becomes a tale of giants doing battle. The fight moves into the sea at Howth and the giants fight so violently the clouds become splattered with blood. This is Irish storytelling at its best. All the modern-day blockbuster movies. from *Harry Potter* to *Lord of the Rings* and the Narnia series (the latter two are from older books) all contain elements of these great ancient tales: giants, goblins, sword fights and a healthy dose of the supernatural where evil has a face and good triumphs. So, without further ado, here are some of the stories that are connected with the valley, in brief.

Fionn, in a poem entitled 'The Hunt of Sliabh Trium', fights and kills monsters, and the story ends with a list of Fionn's greatest victories, one of which is the slaying of the Arrach (the ghostly monster) of Glenasmole.

'The Adventures of Amadán Mór' (The Adventures of the Big Fool) is a story set entirely in the valley and Amadán, who wins a fair maid for his wife, encounters some strange happenings of a supernatural kind. He is told by a *gruagach* (hairy person) that the valley is full of witchcraft. This Amadán discovers for himself, when his legs vanish after drinking from a magic cup. He is led to the *dún* (fort) of Glenasmole which from its description seems extraordinary, a city that shone like gold and other colours the eye has never seen! To quote directly from the story:

'Twas not long till they saw in the valley,
A city that shone like gold,
There was no colour which eye had seen,
That was not in the mansion and many more.

'Twas then the young maiden asked
What golden city is that,
Of the finest appearance and hue,
Or could it be betrayed or traversed?

Dun-an-Oir [Fort of the Gold] is its name
The strong Dun of Glen na Smoil,
There is not now of its inhabitants alive,
But myself and my wife.

The Glen through which thou has passed,
Is always full of witchcraft.

The tale of 'The Chase of Glenasmole' is one of the stories told by Oisín, the son of Fionn Mac Cumhaill, to St Patrick who asks one of his scribes to write them down. It is interesting to note, as the stories are related, that the writers have taken a position against Christianity and refer many times to the way things were better in the old days of the Fianna. They make it obvious that Oisín was not convinced by Patrick and his new Christian ways.

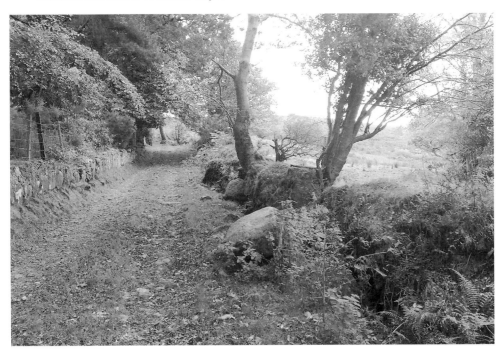

Near Heathfield Lodge and Fionn Mac Cumhaill's stone.

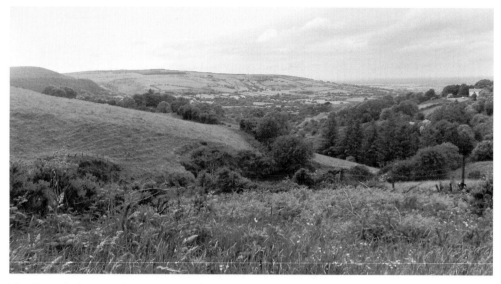

The Fianna's favourite hunting ground.

According to the legend, Fionn, Oisín and the Fianna were out hunting in Glenasmole and Fionn's favourite hound Bran, along with all the other Fianna hounds, was chasing a doe. When cornered, the doe changed into a beautiful woman who announced that she was the daughter of the Supreme King of Greece. She invited them to a feast and offered Fionn, who she addressed as the 'King of the Fianna', her hand in marriage.

Fionn refused and after they ate and drank their fill, the Greek princess (who after being rejected turned into a witch) declared war on the Fianna. She sang a beautiful melody which bewitched everyone in the room and then suddenly drew a sword and cut off the heads of many of the Fianna warriors who were spellbound. In a desperate attempt to prevent any more of his men being decapitated, Fionn told the Greek witch he couldn't marry her because of Goll the Blind, who would not agree to the arrangement. The men were spared and in order to settle this once and for all the entire company set sail to Howth to find Goll.

Goll, wondering where the rest of his warriors were, went into battle with the Greek woman alone. His troops it turned out, were asleep, guarded by fifty women who had cast spells on them. Diarmuid (of the Bright Teeth), who was the only warrior among the sleeping army who hadn't been affected by the enchantment, spoke to a beautiful maid (who was one of the women guarding the sleeping warriors) and told her he would marry her. In her delight, she released the men from their enchantment, but to Diarmuid's horror when one of the Fianna warriors, Conan, woke from the enchantment and realised that this young maid and her accomplices had kept them in pain and prevented them joining the battle with Goll, he was enraged and cut off her head. Diarmuid, who had to be restrained from attacking Conan with his sword, demanded to know why he had done this. Conan justified it with a short and to-the-point speech, giving all, including the reader, a reality check, 'if she was my own daughter or my own mother I would have done the same for what she did'.

They arrived at the place where the battle was still being fought. Oscar relieved Goll and the battle that ensued was of epic proportions: the story tells of the pair cleaving each other to the bone and the clouds being splattered with blood. Oscar, the warrior son of Oisín and the fairy woman Niamh, urged on by the others, triumphed by leaping into the air across all who were watching the fight and lets fly a spear that pierced the heart of the Greek woman. She falls into the sea to her certain death, but just before sinking under the surface of the water she tells them why she came to Ireland, so the story finishes with a twist, leaving everyone feeling a little sympathy for the Greek princess.

Her father, the King of Greece, had put a curse on her to mask her beauty and her form after being told by his druids that they foresaw her son overthrowing Greece and beheading the king. Her last words in the story are as follows:

> Had I but become the wife of a chief or head of hosts, I would give birth to a
> son whom the world would obey
> And I myself would again assume my shape.
> Once I was, though sad my tale,
> Excelling all women, with rolling eyes
> By the wicked druidism of my own father,
> I lost my beauty and my form.

TÍR NA NÓG

On his return from Tír na nÓg (Land of the Young), Oisín rode over the country looking for his old friends. After searching for the Fianna and repeatedly calling for Fionn and Oscar, Bran and Sgeolan in vain, while looking out across the land from the hill of Allen, Oisín remembered their favourite hunting ground ...

Oisín went back down the road and turned the horse's head toward Glenasmole – the Glen of the Thrushes – one of the Fianna's favourite hunting grounds near Dublin. It was in Glenasmole that he saw the first people. A group of men were struggling to move a large rock, and Oisín wondered at this. Any one of the Fianna could have picked the rock up with one hand, and Oscar, Oisín's son and the strong man of the Fianna, could have thrown it over the south side of Glenasmole and landed it on Seefin – the Seat of Fionn – or over the north side of the glen.

Oisín reached down from his horse to help the men lift the stone but the girth of his saddle broke and he fell to the ground. He had been told not to touch the soil of Éireann or he would perish and he instantly aged 300 years (the period of time he had been away).

After his fall the men went to get St Patrick who took Oisín into his care, and after explaining to Oisín that the Fianna had all died out many years before he asked Oisín where he had been all this time. Oisín began to tell the story of Tír na nÓg. St Patrick then put a scribe at Oisín's disposal to write down the stories of the Fianna so they would not be forgotten.

Even though he had aged 300 years, Oisín still had the strength of ten men, which St Patrick put to good use, asking him to clear fields of rocks other men found to heavy too move. Oisín didn't mind this but complained to Patrick about his small meals, saying, 'In my day, I've seen a quarter of a blackbird bigger than your quarter of beef. And I've seen an ivy leaf bigger than your griddle of bread. And I've seen a rowan berry bigger than your churn of butter.'

Patrick didn't believe this and Oisín was so annoyed he set off to Glenasmole again to get an ivy leaf, a blackbird and a rowan berry. (There are records of unusually large ivy that grew at White Cliff and there were rare ferns to be found, such as the *Osmunda Regalis* and the *Hymenophyllum Tunbridgense*.)

Realising that Oisín had been speaking the truth, Patrick apologised to him.

Oisín died in Glenasmole and is said to be buried under the cairn of Ben Edar (Howth) with Aideen, his daughter-in-law, although a contradictory text says he was buried in Antrim at a site known as Oisín's grave.

The most celebrated English-language adaptation of the story of Tír na nÓg was written by Nobel Prize winner William Butler Yeats. His epic poem 'The Wanderings of Oisin' (1889) is one of the early works he didn't disown.

FIONN MAC CUMHAILL'S STONE

Lying at the end of the grounds of Heathfield Lodge, at the corner next the road, there is a granite boulder that once had a marble slab with the following inscription on it:

Finmakoom, one of the Irish Giants, carried this stone on his shoulder from the opposite mountain on April 1st, 1444 – he was 9 feet 7 inches high, and weighed 44 stone.

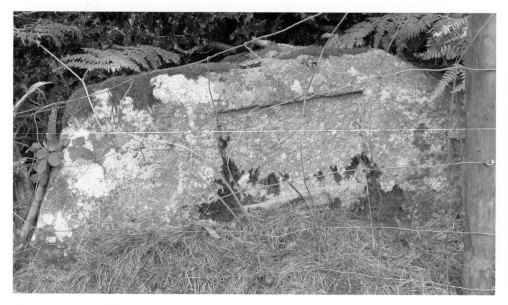

Fionn Mac Cumhaill's Stone near Cobbe's Lodge Glenasmole.

As you can see from the photo, the indentation of the plaque is still in the stone. This stone has been thought to be the same stone as Fionn Mac Cumhaill's finger-stone. The latter was so called from the marks that were said to have been left by the giant's fingers when he threw it from the Hill of Allen to Tallaght.

Fionn's name has been incorporated into local place names, for example Seefinn, which means the 'Seat of Fionn', and Ballymorefinn, which translated becomes 'Fionn's Great Town'.

4

ST SANCTAN

One thousand five hundred years ago two princes were born in northern England. Their father was King Sawyl Penuchel (the Arrogant) of the Southern Pennines, a descendant of Coel Hen immortalised in the nursery rhyme 'Old King Cole'. His first wife, Deichter, was the daughter of King Muiredach Muinderg of Ulster. One of these young princes in later life would have a profound impact on a small valley across the sea in Ireland.

The older prince, Maddock, was born in AD 498 and was brought up at his grandfather's Irish court where he became interested in the Christian religion. He was educated in Leinster before travelling back across the Irish Sea to Glyn Rhosyn, a valley in Pembrokeshire, to study the scriptures under St David.

The younger prince, Sanctan, was born in AD 500. He was inspired by his brother and became an active missionary in Rheged in Cumbria where he founded a number of churches. Several Gaelic saints are recalled in Cumbrian place names, including St Bega, St Brigid, and St Sanctan.

Following in the footsteps of his brother Maddock, who had returned to Ireland (to a monastery on Saint Mogue's Island in Templeport Lake in County Leitrim), Sanctan crossed the Irish Sea, stopping off at the Isle of Man en route, and established the church of Sanctan. Today Kirk Sanctan stands on the site of the 1,500-year-old chapel.

When Sanctan came to Ireland he is said to have been a disciple of St Patrick. Although the dates are slightly out, Sanctan's mother Deichter's family knew the saint all too well. In the 'Tripartite Life of St Patrick' there is a story in which Patrick cursed the descendants of Eochaid (Deichter's uncle) and gave his blessing to the descendants of Eochaid's brother Cairell mac Muiredaig Muinderg after Eochaid had ordered two virgins who wanted to serve God to be drowned. Eochaid's pregnant wife threw herself at Patrick's feet and received baptism in order to spare the curse on her unborn son. Cairell's descendants went on to monopolise the kingship. Sanctan more than likely was inspired by St Patrick and the hymn which Sanctan composed is very obviously influenced by St Patrick's hymn 'The Deer's Cry', better known as 'St Patrick's Breastplate', in which the saint invokes the protection of God. Both hymns are preserved in the *Liber Hymnorum of Ireland* Vol. II.

Sanctan composed the hymn as he travelled from Clonard to Templeport Lake in County Leitrim. According to the Manuscript of St Isidore: 'The cause of

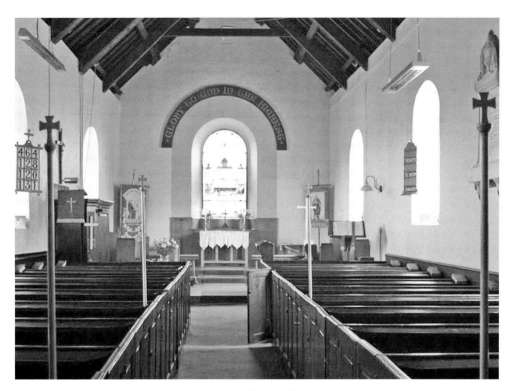

St Sanctan was changed to St Anne in the Isle of Man also but they have reverted to the old saint's name.

the composition of this poem was that he might be preserved from his enemies, and that his brother might admit him amongst the religious in the island. At that time he had no knowledge of the Irish language but God miraculously granted it to him.'

He subsequently became Bishop Sanctan and founded two churches, Cill-da-Les and Kilnasantan in Glassamucky, County Dublin in the sixth century (mentioned in the *Book of Leinster*). Cill-da-Les, which means 'church of two forts', has not been identified. The *Annals of the Four Masters* record the death of one of the abbots at St Sanctan's in Kilnasantan in the year 952, that's 450 years approximately after it was founded.

As early as the middle of the seventeenth century Post Reformation, Sanctan was confused with St Anne (the mother of the Virgin Mary) and both the church in the Isle of Man and the church and monastery at Kilnasantan became known as St Anne's and so the story of this pioneering saint was lost in time. This was, however, noticed and officially corrected in the Isle of Man in 1891 and the parish is now once again rightfully St Sanctan's.

Professor Joyce records that, in the county of Dublin, 'there is a picturesque little graveyard and ruin called Kill St. Ann, near it is St. Ann's Well and an adjacent residence has borrowed from the church the name of Ann Mount.' Irish records show that its ancient name was *Cill Easpuig Sanctáin*, 'the church of Bishop Sanctan.'

St Sanctan is one of the early saints. His feast day is on 20 May.

THE HYMN OF ST SANCTAN

I beseech the wonderful King of Angels,
For his is the name that is mightiest;
God be with me on my track, God on my left,
God before me, God on my right.

God to help me, O holy invocation!
Against every danger that I encounter;
Let there be a bridge of life under me,
The blessing of God the Father over me.

May the Noble Trinity awaken him,
For whom a good death is not in store.
The Holy Spirit, the Strength of Heaven
God the Father, the great Son of Mary.

May the great King, who knows our crimes
God of the noble sinless world,
Be with my soul against every sin of falsity,
That the torment of demons may not touch me.

May God repel every sadness from me;
May Christ relieve my sufferings;
May the Apostles be around me,
May the Trinity of witness come to me.

May a flood of mercy come from Christ,
Whose wounds are not hidden (from us):
Let not death touch me,
Nor bitterness, nor plague, nor disease.

Let not a sharp cast touch me
Apart from God's Son, who gladdens and who mortifies:
Let Christ protect me against every iron-death,
Against fire, against the raging sea.

Against every death-pool that is dangerous
To my body, with awful storms,
May God at every hour be with me,
Against the wind, against the swift waters.

I will utter the praises of Mary's Son,
Who battles our white battles,
May God of the elements answer;
A corslet in battle shall be my prayer.

Whilst praying to God of the Heavens,
Let my body be enduring penitent,
That I may not go to awful Hell
I beseech the King whom I have besought.

Bishop Sanctain [Sanctan], illustrious father,
Angel-soldier of bright, pure fame;
My body being freed on earth,
May he receive my soul in Heaven.

Offer a prayer for me, O Mary!
That the heavenly mercy may be shown to us:
Against wounding, against danger, against suffering,
O Christ, afford us thy protection.

I implore the noble, everlasting king;
May the Only-begotten of God plead for us;
Against sharp torments, may
The Son who was born in Bethlehem defend me.

KILNASANTAN

Kilnasantan is the English renaming of *Cill-na-Sanctan* ('Church of Sanctan').
This illustrates how the name Sanctan became St Ann when it was renamed
during the Reformation; this phonetic translation can be seen in most of the old

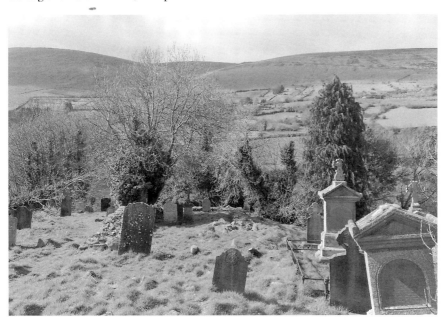

This was a druid burial ground before Sanctan.

place names. Sanctan's name was spelt in various ways over the years, which makes searching for information difficult. The most popular versions are with or without the 'c'; I have left it in as I chose to keep the older spelling and also to avoid confusion in the text.

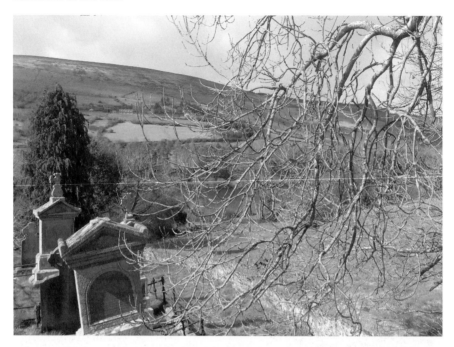

Above and below: Kilnasantan, the 1,500-year-old church, now in ruin, and the ancient graveyard.

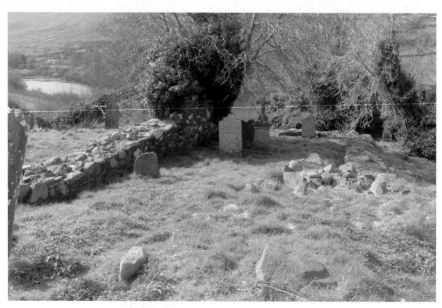

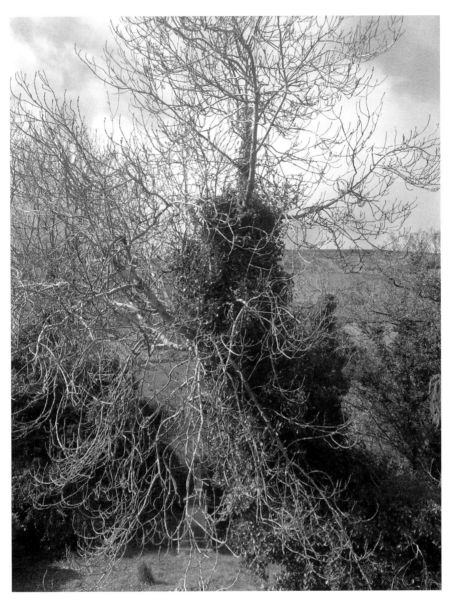

A close-up of the unusual tree growing out of the ruined church wall.

The church was founded by St Sanctan, as recorded in the *Book of Leinster*. The *Annals of the Four Masters* later record the death of one of its abbots, Caenchom-raic, in the year 952. Archbishop Comyn, who built and endowed St Patrick's Cathedral in Dublin, granted Kilnasantan to the College of St Patrick and confirmation of that grant was made by a Bull of Pope Celestine III in 1191. In 1216 Pope Innocent III confirmed it to the See of Dublin and it was constituted a manor from which the archbishop received rent from the tenants and profits from the demesne land.

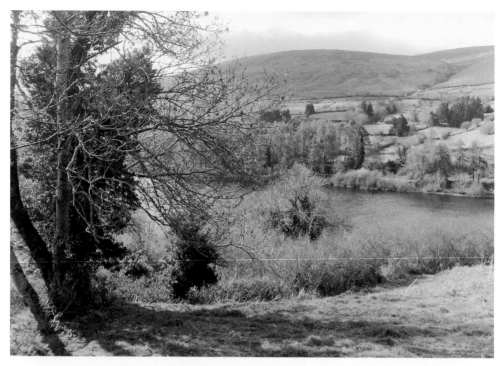

View of the Bohernabreena reservoir from St Sanctan's.

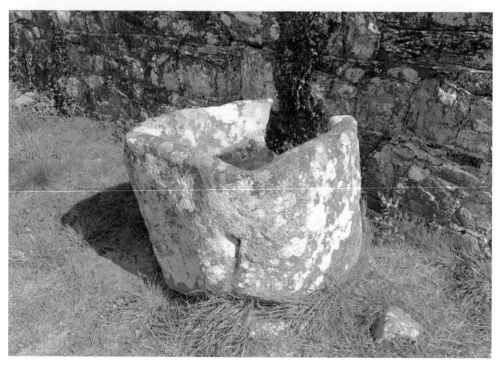

The remains of the early Christian font in the graveyard of St Sanctan's church.

The archbishop's portion of the lands was comprised in two areas, Kilnasantan and Brittas (possibly the church of Kilbride near Blessington). In addition to rents from freeholders, betaghs* and cottagers, and profits from demesne lands, the archbishop received from Kilnasantan 'a customary cow', and from Brittas a tribute of beer and meat. These demands were not well received by tenants and in 1276 it was necessary to employ Sheriff John de Peter with five armed horsemen and fifteen followers as well as the bailiff and posse of Clondalkin to keep the peace in the mountains of Kilnasantan. The church was later devastated during a battle in 1294.

In 1326 the lands of Kilnasantan, which had been partly held under the archbishop by the Priory of St John of Jerusalem' (The Priory were a branch of the Knights Templar) were returned as being in the Irish territory and therefore worthless. 1541 Kilnasantan was rebuilt and used again.

In the next century English residents were to be found in the valley and, after the rebellion of 1641, two of them made depositions which show that they were substantial farmers. This is all the more surprising given that Irish was the language spoken in the area. In 1672 there is a reference to repairs to the church. Soon afterwards, because the location of Sanctan's was inconvenient, a chapel was erected at Templeogue (*Temple-Oge*, meaning 'New Church'); thus St Sanctan's church ceased to be a place of worship and sadly went to ruin.

*A betagh was a peasant who gave dues and services to a lord in exchange for land. They were not slaves, and were named as freemen and freewomen in medieval documents, but they were not free. They and their land and possessions belonged to the lord of the manor. They were not free to leave the manor and they were subject to a large number of obligations required by the lord, including work on the lord's demesne two or three days a week, additional work at harvest, and the payment of manorial dues.

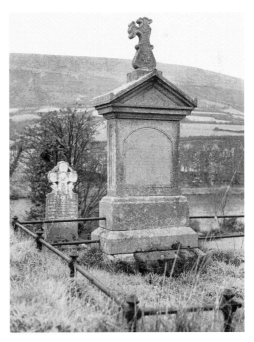

Sanctan's gaveyard in 1976.
(Courtesy of South County Dublin Library)

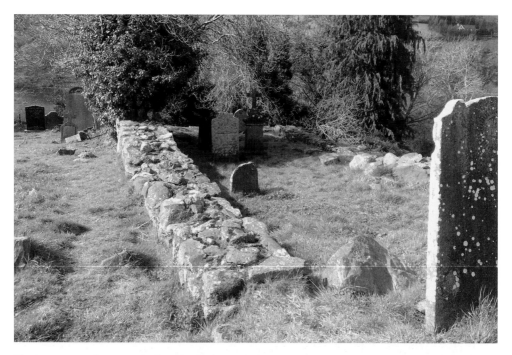

The remnants of Sanctan's church, the rectangular outline of the walls still visible after all these years.

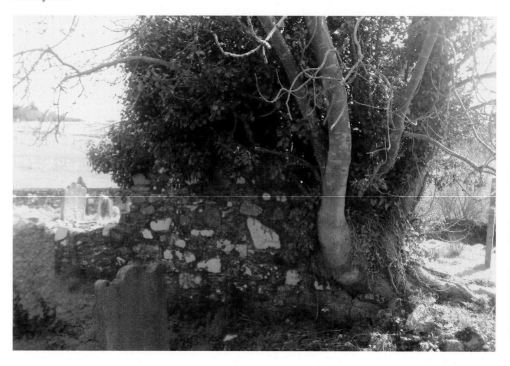

The highest-standing remnant of the church wall.

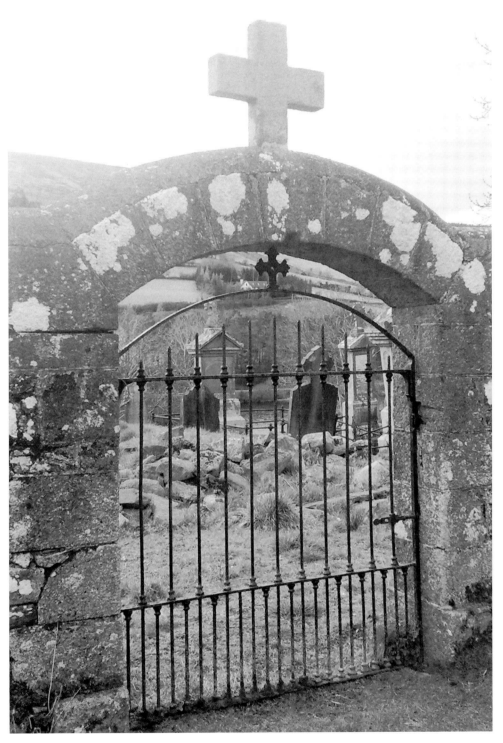

The gates of St Sanctan's graveyard (one of the oldest graveyards in Ireland) and church.

ST ANNE'S WELL

Close to the site of St Sanctan's church and overlooking the reservoir is St Anne's Well, as it is known now, or the Holy Well of Kilnasantan. The well is surrounded by a granite wall, which is only noticeable up close as grass covers it now. In the old days this well was always visited on the feast of St Anne (26 July). People had great belief in the healing properties of the well water. It was said to cure sore eyes and stomach pains. As was the custom at the time, beads, medals, coins or ribbon were hung or tied to the branches of the rowan tree that overhang the well. There are records of two other holy wells, one at Ballymore Finn and another at Allagour.

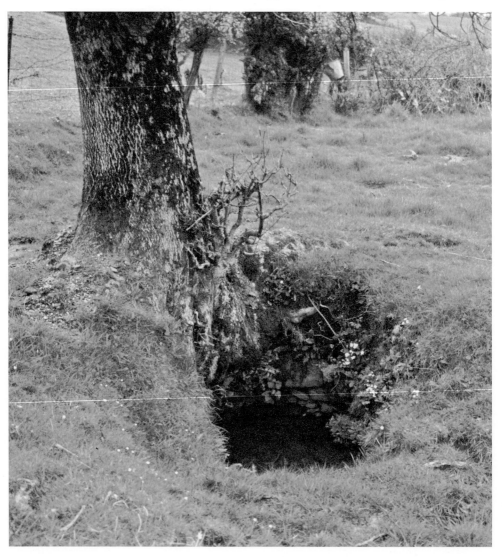

St Sanctan's holy well, now known as St Anne's, at Kilnasantan. (Courtesy of South County Dublin Library)

5

THE ROYAL OAKS
OF GLENCREE

TO THE OAKS OF GLENCREE

My arms are round you, and I lean
Against you, while the lark
Sings over us, and golden lights, and green
Shadows are on your bark.

There'll come a season when you'll stretch
Black boards to cover me;
Then in Mount Jerome I will lie, poor wretch,
With worms eternally.

John Millington Synge, 1871–1909

As early as the eleventh century the Irish oak forests were well known to the English, as is shown by a request said to have been made by William Rufus for Irish oak for the building of Westminster Hall. Giraldus Cambrensis mentions in his book, *The Topography of Ireland*, that there was an excess of wood and very little open ground. There was a forest at Glencree but it only formed a small part of the wide-spreading forests alluded to by Holinshed and Spenser, who tell us that the Wicklow glens were full of great trees on the sides of the hills. Where did it all go? Well, the answer follows.

Just beyond Kippure and outside the area of the valley there was the Royal Oak Forest of Glencree. In the early days of the English occupation, when the forest laws of the Normans were still rigidly enforced and the hunt chase was the most popular sport, preservation of the natural forests became an important function of the government.

Glencree was almost entirely covered by oak forest and probably enclosed by some sort of artificial boundary (presumably similar to Phota Island in Cork)

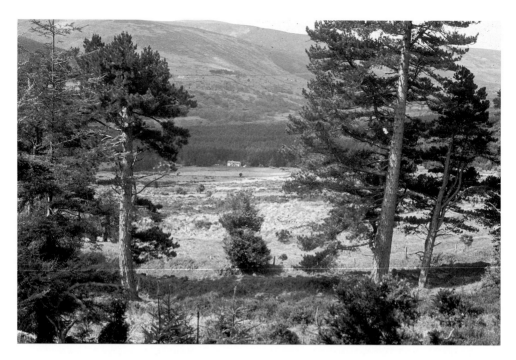

Glencree, once the location of the Royal Game Park, now stripped of its oak forests. (Courtesy of South County Dublin Library)

to prevent the game animals from wandering away into the wilds of Wicklow. In *Sweetman's Calendar* it is recorded that in 1244 eighty deer were sent from the Royal Forest at Chester to stock the king's park at Glencree, and that in 1296 the king sent a present to Eustace le Peer of twelve deer from the Glencree forest. The government supplied wardens or gamekeepers in order to protect the royal preserve and prevent poaching.

The monks of St Mary's Abbey (which was between Kilternan and Glencullen) were unable to resist the temptation of the forest. The chartulary of the abbey in 1291 noted that the abbot was attacked for hunting in the forest. He had with him greyhounds and what are described as 'implements of the chase'.

The Justiciary Rolls of Edward I in 1305 contain an entry states that Thomas de Sandely a carpenter, was kept for three weeks in irons in Dublin Castle after being charged with stealing timber by John Mathew who was the Royal Forester at Glencree. He was caught in the act, but escaped and fled to Dublin, where he was later arrested.

In 1283 William le Deveneis, keeper of the king's demesne lands, was granted twelve oaks fit for timber from the king's wood in 'Glincry', (the old spelling of Glencree) and a few years later, Queen Eleanor, wife of Edward I, established large timber works in the valley for the purpose of providing wood for her castle, then being built at Haverford in Wales. William de Moines (one of the family from which Rathmines derives its name) was keeper and manager of the timber works, and, judging by reports in the State Papers of the work carried out, a huge amount of the timber was cut down during this period.

As time went on, the royal passion for the hunt chase started to wane and the authorities began to see this great forest in a different light, on account of the shelter afforded to criminals, who were able to hide out in the woods. In the State Papers of Elizabeth I the woods are described as 'a shelter for all ill-disposed' and 'the seat and nursery of rebellion'. It was suggested that the woods should be cleared and then the land rented, or that the trees should be burnt down to make wide paths through the woods so as to make it harder for criminals to hide, and easier for the authorities to patrol the area. Eventually the Government adopted the surest and most profitable strategy, the establishment of iron works in all the great forest districts, and there were many around the country. The iron works at the time were fuelled by timber so there was plenty of raw material. However, no iron works was established at Glencree due to the rebel activity there.

No further records of the Glencree Royal forest can be discovered after this, and it seems probable that in consequence of the withdrawal of numbers of English from Ireland for the purpose of the war in Scotland, and to join Edward I's expedition to Flanders, the forest had to be abandoned. In any case, it is pretty certain that no successful attempt could have been made to hold it during the rising of the Irish tribes, the general disturbances around the country which followed the invasion of the Bruces a few years later and the rebellion in Leinster in 1301–2.

Later the English Government awoke to the destruction caused by the exportation of timber and its waste in minor uses, and the Lords of the Council gave orders, in 1609, that the timber growing in the king's woods should be reserved for building and repairing the king's ships.

6

STONE CROSS AND MASS ROCK

The Act of Supremacy and Uniformity in 1560, the Cromwellian period and Penal Laws were a terrible time for our ancestors and for the Catholic Church in Ireland. On 6 January 1653, the four parliamentary commissioners for the affairs of Ireland issued from Dublin a decree banishing Catholic priests. Within twenty days of this date all priests were to present themselves to the authorities to express their

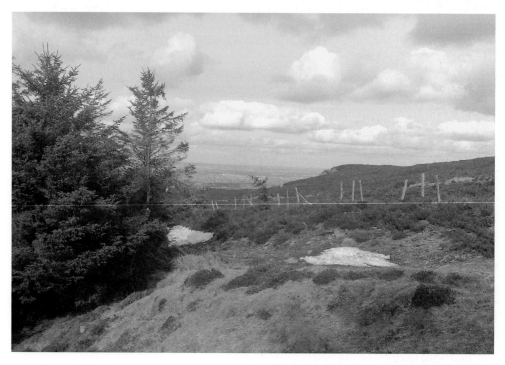

The view from the Mass Rock, looking towards Dublin, This was taken in early April 2010 and snow is visible on the pathway.

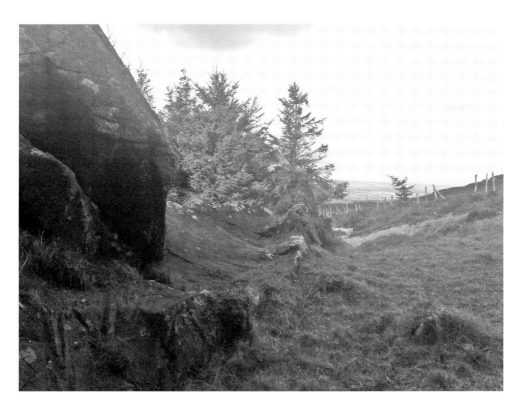

Above: The Mass Rock.

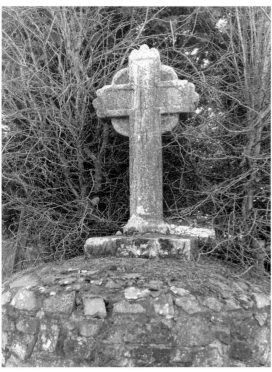

Left: The stone cross at Ballinascorney.

willingness to be transported overseas at the earliest opportunity. Failure to comply rendered a priest guilty of high treason, for which the penalty was death. Many old and sick priests obeyed and went abroad, but others ignored the decree and went into hiding. Some were caught and executed. It became a matter of life and death to say mass or to attend.

It is because of this that the 'Mass Rock' became the new place of worship. The mass was held in a place completely hidden from view, usually in a hollow at the top of a hill. In Ballinascorney, off the road to Kilbride Camp on Seehan Mountain, the mass rock is still there for all to see. The congregation had a great view over the landscape below and lookouts were posted to watch out for the dreaded 'priest hunters'.

The priest would arrive on foot, sometimes in disguise (if the people were interrogated they could honestly say they didn't know who the priest was) and he would wait on the hill top for his flock to arrive. People would sneak up the hill through the forest, but not all together; it had to be done in complete secrecy. There are two streams, Swiftbrook and Corrig brook, which people would walk through so there would be no trace of their footprints, especially when there was snow. As you can imagine, the water would have been incredibly cold. When all had arrived mass would be celebrated.

Mass is still celebrated at the Mass Rock in Ballinascorney each year, in memory of both priests and the parishioners who risked their lives to receive the sacraments.

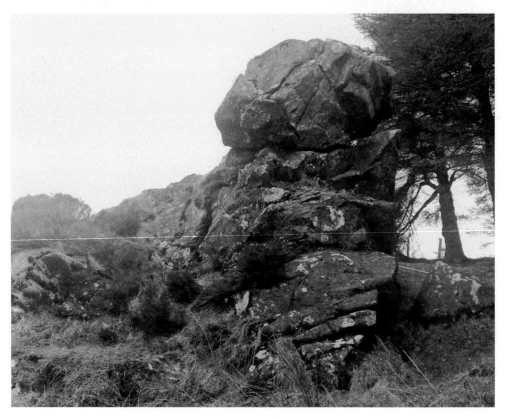

The Mass Rock, also known as Cloway Rock, at Ballinascorney.

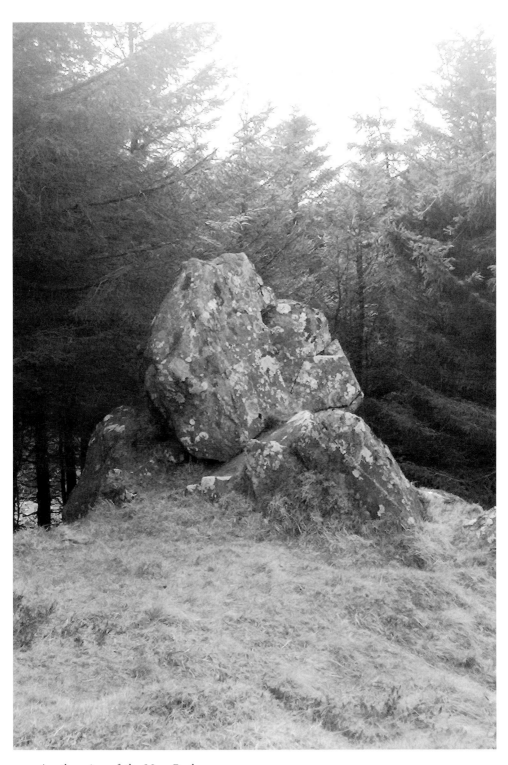

Another view of the Mass Rock.

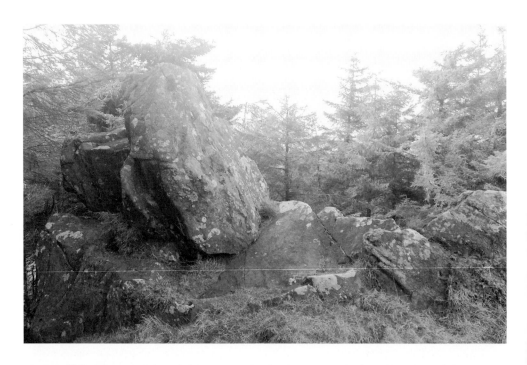

Above and below: Two pictures of the Mass Rock. The flat area at the bottom centre of the pictures is where the priest would set the altar.

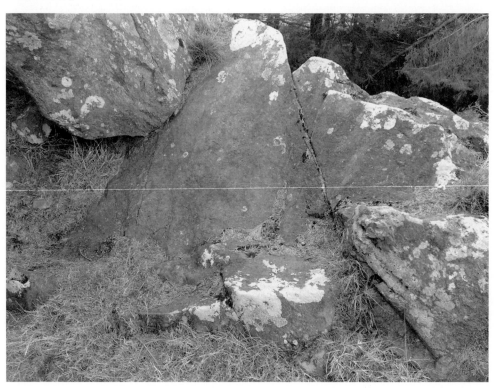

7

MONTPELIER HILL

Montpelier Hill was named as such by Speaker Conolly when he took possession of it in the early eighteenth century. The Irish name is alas unknown but possibilities include *Suide Uí Ceallaig* or *Suidi Celi*, the latter being mentioned in the *Crede Mihi* of the twelfth century.

Conolly built a lodge on the hill about the year 1725. According to local legend, an ancient cromlech or cairn erected to the old pagan gods of Ireland was demolished to make way for the lodge. It is said the roof was first slated, but the wind blew the slates off. The people said the devil would never let a roof remain on it, in consequence of the desecration of the cairn. Squire Conolly would, however, not be conquered by devil or wind. He built an arched roof with large

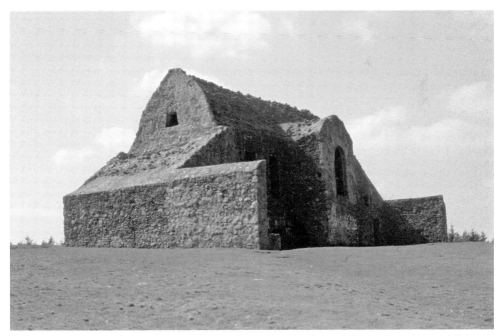

Montpelier Lodge, one of the headquarters of the Dublin Hellfire Club. (Courtesy of South County Dublin Library)

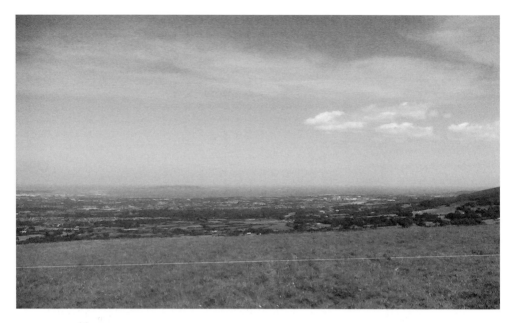

View from the Hellfire Club, looking towards Dublin City with Howth just visible in the distance.

stones placed edgeways, and filed to a smooth surface with smaller stones and mortar. This was done so well that much of it remains to the present day, in spite of its exposed situation and lack of repairs.

There was a large deer-park on Montpelier, enclosed by the Conolly family. There was also one at this time at Ballinascorney. No doubt, these deer-parks were well stocked and it must have been a grand sight when a meet of the hounds took place in the beautiful lawn in front of Lord Ely's hunting lodge, then surrounded by woods. The nobles and ladies would make their way up the steep avenue behind the house, and over the hills, to the glen at the back of it, under Featherbed Bog. Here they would probably start some outlying stag, and the chase would lead over the hills and valleys of Glenasmole, rivalling the legendary stories of the Finnian hunts celebrated in old Irish poems.

Joseph Holt, the insurgent general, records in his memoirs that in July 1798, during the retreat of the rebels from County Meath, he passed safely through Dublin and spent the night in the haunted house (the lodge) on Montpelier. He wrote, 'I lay down in the arched room of that remarkable building. I felt confident of the protection of the Almighty that the name of enchantment and the idle stories that were told of the place had but a slight hold of my mind.'

In spite of his perilous situation he was deeply impressed by the beauty of the sunrise as seen from this position. He sent a message to his brother who lived in Chapel House, Bohernabreena, requesting a loaf of bread, some cheese and a pint of whiskey.

The roof was much damaged in 1849, when Queen Victoria was in Dublin and a great number of tar barrels were set on fire. It made a great bonfire that could be seen from the city, but split many of the stones.

THE HELLFIRE CLUB

At the beginning of the eighteenth century, a time of sharp contrast between the fabulously wealthy and the destitute, there lived a class of gentry called 'bucks' who spent their lives pursuing enjoyment in a most violent and eccentric manner. Their behaviour was viewed at the time as an insult to the most sacred principles of religion, an affront to Almighty God himself, and corrupting to the minds and morals of young people. This life consisted, it is said, of gambling, blaspheming, whoring, drinking, violence and even Satanism.

Colonel Jack St Leger, as his name suggests, had deep sporting instincts and his country house near Athy in County Kildare was the haunt of the leading gamblers and racing men of the day. Huge amounts of money changed hands at parties here, and vast quantities of liquor were consumed. It was in this atmosphere that, along with Richard Parsons, 1st Earl of Rosse, he founded the Dublin Hellfire Club. Its motto was 'do as you will'.

The club had various headquarters around Dublin such as the now-demolished Eagle Tavern on Cork Hill. On occasion at the Eagle, members would sit around a circular table upon which was placed a huge punch bowl of scaltheen, a rancid mixture of Irish whiskey and melted butter. After toasting the Devil and drinking to the 'damnation of the Church and its prelates' the bucks would pour scaltheen over a cat, specially obtained for the occasion, and set fire to the poor creature. Once a flaming cat escaped and ran into the street, causing panic outside the tavern.

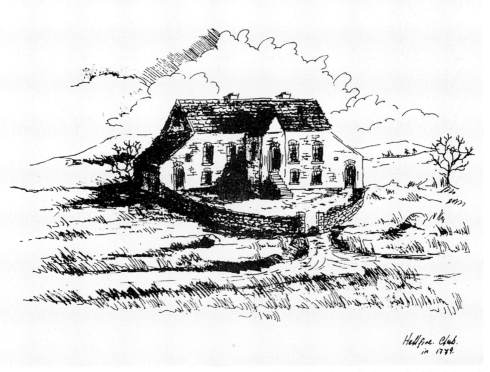

Hellfire Club.
in 1779.

The Hellfire Club in 1779 by an unknown artist. (Courtesy of South County Dublin Library)

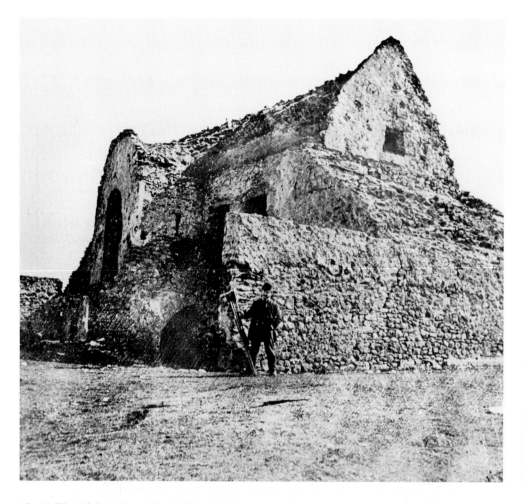

The Hellfire Club in the early 1900s.

Another favourite meeting place was Daly's Club, College Green. Here the shutters were closed in the morning so that members with hangovers could continue to gamble by candlelight. One gruesome incident occurred when a member, said to be 'Buck' Sheely, was caught cheating at cards. A 'court' was convened presided over by 'Buck' English who dressed for the part in the skin, tail and horns of a bull. His verdict was that Sheely was to be hurled through the window of the third-floor gaming room. When honour had been satisfied, gambling was resumed. Sheely died in the fall.

Their final, and best-known, headquarters was the lodge on Montpelier Hill. The remoteness of the location well suited the bucks and its commanding view of Dublin had a powerful appeal to their insufferable arrogance. For at least twenty years Montpelier Lodge flourished as a den of all kinds of vice and blasphemy until it was ruined by the bucks themselves around 1740.

The 'principal' of the Hellfire Club was a man of enormous wealth called Richard Chappell Whaley. A descendant of Oliver Cromwell, Whaley was a tyrant who was feared and hated by the local people. His nickname was 'Burn-Chapel' Whaley because of his fanatical hatred of religion in general and Roman Catholicism in particular. He was a priest hunter, and on Sundays, for his amusement, he would ride around the district setting fire to the thatched Catholic chapels, which became

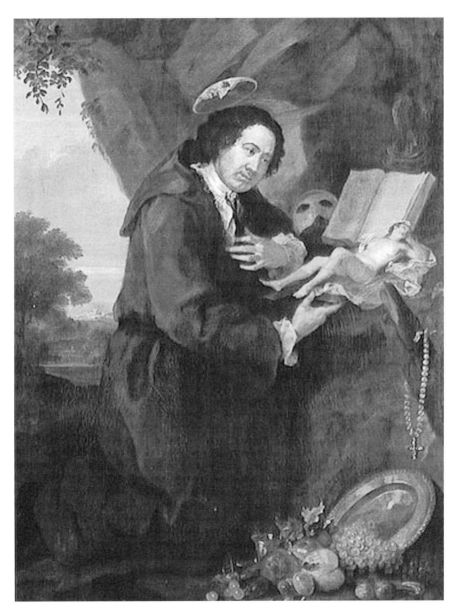

Portrait of Francis Dashwood, 15th Baron le Despencer by William Hogarth from the late 1750s, parodying Renaissance images of Francis of Assisi. The Bible has been replaced by a copy of the erotic novel *Elegantiae Latini Sermonis*, and the profile of Dashwood's friend Lord Sandwich peers from the halo.

the places of worship after the laws were relaxed and mass rocks were no longer used. It was his pyromania that caused the downfall of Montpelier Lodge.

The story of the disaster is well known. After an unfrocked clergyman had performed a Black Mass in one of the two upstairs rooms in the lodge, the ceremony ended in the usual drunken revelry. A footman, picking his way through the sprawling bodies, spilt some drink on Richard Whaley's coat. Whaley reacted by pouring brandy over the footman and setting him alight. The man fled downstairs clutching at a tapestry hanging by the hall door, trying to douse the flames. Within minutes the whole building was ablaze. Many bucks died, being too drunk and helpless to escape. Whaley managed to leap out of a window along with a few of his more sober companions.

Another version of the tale tells of a stranger at the Hellfire who joined a game of cards and soon was doing well as he had quickly amassed a large amount of money. The gamblers wondered who this stranger was. At one stage during the game a player dropped a card on the floor and bent down to pick it up but something caught his eye; as he looked across at the stranger he was horrified to see he had hooves instead of feet. He jumped up suddenly, shouting that he had seen the devil and, becoming hysterical, threw over the gaming table. Cards, money, drinks and candles slid to the floor and a blaze ensued which caught a tapestry and the building went up in flames. This story has gone round the world, published in many horror novels and compilations of ghost stories.

BUCK WHALEY

Born in 1766, Thomas 'Buck' Whaley was elected to the Irish House of Commons at the age of 18, standing for Newcastle in Dublin, a seat he held until 1790. He had very little to say about parliamentary life in his memoirs; it was his other life that made him the infamous character that is remembered to this day.

'Buck' Whaley took the Hellfire Club from the low ebb to which it had sunk after the burning of Montpelier Lodge to new heights, declaring his intention of 'defying God and man in nightly revels'. Black Masses and drunken orgies were the principal features of these sessions and though Whaley himself had a mistress, he kept her well away from these meetings.

'Buck' Whaley initially squandered the fortune he inherited from his father, but then he won an even greater fortune at the gaming tables as well as inventing bizarre wagers. In one wager, which began as a joke over dinner with the Duke of Leinster in Leinster House, Whaley agreed to walk to Jerusalem and back within a year. The bet was probably his most famous. He set out with a friend, Captain Wilson, in 1789. Needless to say, Whaley was not on a pilgrimage and he later boasted of having 'drunk his way around the Holy Places' and 'played hand ball at the Wailing Wall'. He returned to Dublin a year later to crowds and bonfires in the streets celebrating his win. As proof Whaley had a certificate signed by a superior of the Convent of Nazareth. But after spending two years gambling and drinking in Daly's Club on Stephen's Green he was in debt again.

He seemed to come up with ideas to raise money for himself no matter what the consequences, and for a bet of £12,000 he rode a beautiful Arab stallion in a death-defying leap from the drawing room of his father's house on Stephen's Green to the street some 30ft below. He won his wager but killed the horse. (His brother-in-law told the story in his memoirs and noted that Whaley was crippled for life afterwards.)

Tired of Dublin, he went to London and bought horses and carriages and took out memberships in all the fashionable clubs. He became a man about town in the West End and was in Paris for the French Revolution. He fled Paris after accusing a count of cheating in a game of cards and ended up in Dublin again where he sold off his estates and paid his debts. This left him with £5,000, which (in true style) he decided to gamble. Throwing his lot to faith he reasoned he would make a handsome fortune or he would be ruined. In his memoirs Whaley claimed to have spent £400,000 in his lifetime and ended up £30,000 in debt and, he wrote, 'in all that time I never purchased an hour of true happiness'.

But Whaley was in luck; a year after he purchased a seat in parliament as MP for Enniscorthy (1798), the Act of Union was presented to the house. Whaley was bribed by both sides for his vote. He received £4,000 from one side and a blank cheque from the other!

Contrition and remorse, however, began to enter into Whaley's mind and so he resolved to seek absolution for his sins. While kneeling in the darkened nave in St Audoen's church he had a vision of the Devil creeping down the aisle towards him. Seized with terror, Whaley ran from the church and fled Ireland forever. He lived the last few years of his life, with his mistress, in a spectacular mansion he built in Douglas on the Isle of Man, which later became the Fort Anne Hotel. The building was demolished in the 1990s and rebuilt in 1998 in similar style. While he lived there he played cards regularly with the Prince of Wales and won large sums of money which kept him in the style he was accustomed to.

He died at the age of 34 of sclerosis of the liver. In his memoirs, a repentant 'Buck' Whaley wrote that he felt,

> no trifling sensation from the prospect that this simple narrative may persuade the young and inexperienced, if the language of truth has the power of persuasion that a life of dissipation can produce no enjoyment, and that tumultuous pleasures afford no real happiness.

With his death the Dublin Hellfire Club ceased to exist.

8

HEATHFIELD

The English episcopal family of Cobbe first arrived in Ireland in 1717 and Charles Cobbe became Archbishop of Dublin in 1742. He established the Newbridge estate, built the magnificent Newbridge House in North Dublin and purchased and passed on to his family much of the traditional Church lands, which included Glenasmole. In 1755 Cobbe leased to his son, Thomas, the mountain town and lands of Glasnamucky, Ballyslater, Kilnasantan, and Castlekelly. Thomas, in turn, let a portion of land to George Grierson, who built Heathfield around 1792. In 1857 the estate was back in the possession of the Cobbe family and Heathfield became known as Cobbe's Lodge.

The great-grandson of Archbishop Cobbe was Charles Cobbe (1781–1857), who kept extensive diaries chronicling the life of a rural landlord and his tenants. He took over the management of the settlements in the valley of Glenasmole and sold off family paintings in order to build eighty stone and slate cottages for his tenants. He reformed the way property was managed by a landlord and kept his rents low. He sold produce on to the city and it was these links with traders in Meath Street that saved the valley from the ravages of the famine.

Cobbe's daughter, Francis Power Cobbe, wrote a number of books and founded the Society for the Protection of Animals in 1875, the world's first organisation campaigning against animal experiments, still active today. She was also a member of the executive council of the London National Society for Women's Suffrage and writer of editorial columns for London newspapers on suffrage, property rights for women, and opposition to vivisection.

The Cobbe family are representative of the new English planters who dominated politics and the economic life of the country from around 1650 to 1900. They can be regarded as local absentees from Glenasmole but their influence is very pronounced in the valley's geography.

Recently a portrait of William Shakespeare was discovered in the art collection in Newbridge House. The painting dates back to 1610 and has been in the Cobbe family collection for centuries.

HEATHFIELD LODGE (CASTLEKELLY/ COBBE'S LODGE)

Heathfield Lodge, or Cobbe's Lodge as it was later known when the Cobbe family resided here, is situated at the head of the glen. Originally built by George Grierson, it was timber-framed with a thatched roof and a balcony of carved woodwork.

George Grierson was the King's Printer and grandson of George Grierson, who, in 1709, had a printing office in Essex Street, at the sign of the Two Bibles. Among his productions were the first edition published in Ireland, in 1724, of *Paradise Lost*. Sir William Petty's *Maps of Ireland* and a beautifully bound *Book of Common Prayer*, traditionally believed to have been used in the Irish House of Commons are now preserved in the National Library.

Grierson's wife, Constantia, was regarded as one of the most learned scholars of her age. She was fluent in Hebrew, Greek, Latin, French and other languages, was a good mathematician and wrote elegantly in verse and prose. Grierson, through the influence of Lord Carteret, then Viceroy, obtained, in 1727, a reversion of the patent office of King's Printer in Ireland, which gave him full power and authority for the sole imprinting of religious books and statutes. The life of his wife was included in the patent, in recognition of her talents. Mrs Grierson edited several classical works, which were greatly esteemed. She died in 1733 at the early age of 27.

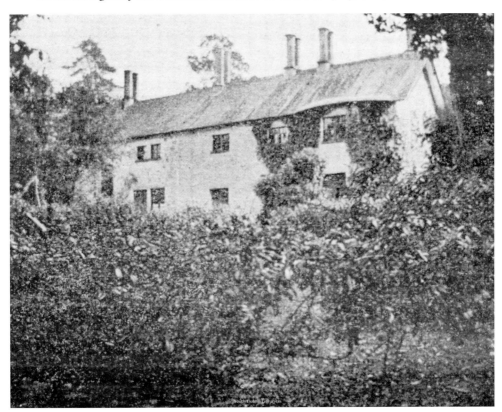

Cobbe's Lodge taken from the book *The Neighbourhood of Dublin* by Weston St John Joyce (1905). (Courtesy of South County Dublin Library)

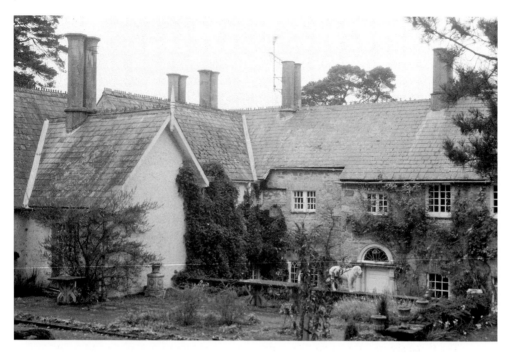

Above and below: More recent photographs of the lodge. (Courtesy of South County Dublin Library)

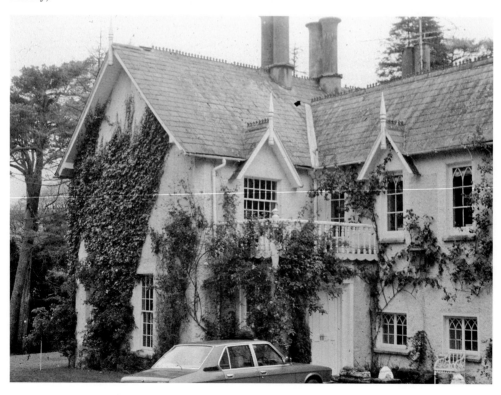

Grierson (the grandson) is stated to have had an income of about £20,000 a year before the Act of Union. During the shooting season he entertained numerous nobility and gentry at Heathfield. It is said that he had six complete dinner services, one for each day, and all were cleaned up on Saturday, ready for the next week. Grierson was said to be a very convivial old gentleman, who sang a good song, was very witty, and behaved as a first-rate host. At the time of the Union he received £13,000 compensation for the termination of his office as publisher of the *Dublin Gazette*, all of which he expended. He built Woodtown House at Mount Venus, where he had a model farm and was very successful in gaining prizes for his cattle and crops, but at an enormous cost. He had also a fine house at Rathfarnham, now the Loreto Convent, and another house in Harcourt Street.

Notwithstanding all his wealth, he died several thousand pounds in debt, which his sons John and George very honourably paid off. After his death, his three daughters lived for many years at Heathfield Lodge. Regular visitors to the lodge were Grierson's sons, who started the *Daily Express*. They spent all their own, as well as their sisters', money on the enterprise. John was a particularly colourful character who would drive his spring-cart furiously from the city. When travelling after dark he gave a double warning of his approach to clear the way using a powerful lamp mounted on the cart and blowing an immense trumpet every 100 yards.

The three sisters were great travellers, and visited many parts of the world, at a time when it was unusual for ladies to journey so extensively. They brought back numerous curiosities from their travels and their home became quite a museum; the polished floors were covered with the skins of wild beasts, antlers of every kind hung round the walls and the tables were loaded with curiosities. Outside the doors were mats made of heather in blossom, renewed daily. The garden contained many rare plants and magnificent rhododendrons.

They were respected and beloved by all who knew them and the people of the glen looked up to them with the devotion of the old Irish to their chiefs. In return the sisters spent much of their time in teaching and visiting them and in helping any of the young people who showed superior intellect. They introduced woodcarving in the Swiss style and beautiful specimens of the handiwork of some of their protégés still exist.

An accidental fire destroyed the house but luckily the ladies escaped to a loft over a detached barn. From there they watched the destruction of all their treasures. George Grierson had the lodge rebuilt to a plan he had drawn himself, modelled on a Swiss chalet but with a slate roof.

His brother John married a Miss Skene, a daughter of Sir Walter Scott's friend, to whom one of the cantos of *Marmion* was dedicated. His eldest son George was subsequently drowned while on a voyage to Natal, and John himself died in Syria.

In the middle of the eighteenth century 'hedge schools' were held by a travelling teacher near Glenasmole Lodge. Later one of the Grierson brothers set up the first school for girls; boys also attended up to the age of nine. If any boys wished to study religion they were sent to Anne Mount. The school Grierson had provided was thatched and during a violent storm one night the roof was blown off and a galvanised roof put on. Later there were two schools, one for boys and one for girls in Glenasmole. Each school had two teachers. The children, who walked to school, came from as far away as upper Ballinascorney, Old Bawn and Killakee. There was a fire grate in each school but fuel was never provided, except for a few bags which were collected once a year at the church door. Most of the children who lived nearby always brought along a sod of turf or a brasskin or sticks but it was only the infants, who sat closer, who got any heat from the fire. During Lent rabbits and ling were dried by the fire.

The Cobbe family took the house back and rebuilt it and it became known as Cobbe's Lodge. It has changed hands many times since.

9

ALLENTON HOUSE

Allenton House was an attractive two-storey, five-bay building in the classical style built in the early eighteenth century. It was castellated and had a curious narrow square tower. Situated on the Oldcourt Road, the house was named for Sir Timothy Allen who was Lord Mayor of Dublin in 1762/1763. In the *Dublin Journal* of 24–27 July 1762, it was announced that 'Last Saturday evening our worthy Lord Mayor, coming from his country seat at Temple-Oge, the horse took fright, and ran into a ditch, by which his lordship was very much cut and bruised; but we have the pleasure of assuring the public his wounds are no way dangerous. His lady, who was in the chaise, received but little hurt.' There is a monument to him in St Maelruain's church, and the grounds

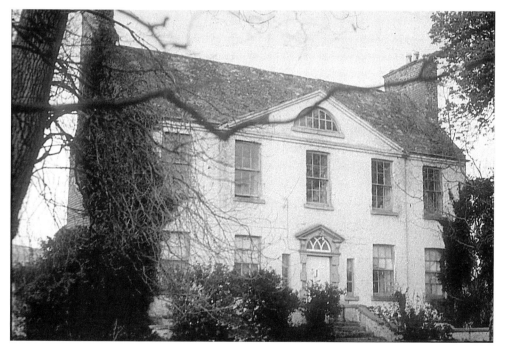

Allenton House, built on the site of an ancient church monastery. (Courtesy of South County Dublin Library)

of Allenton had walnut trees supposed to be associated with St Maelruain's tree at Tallaght.

Allenton was owned in turn by the Norman de Ridelford family followed by the De Merisco family and after them the Ashbournes. It was built on the site of an ancient church and monastic community. According to legend, these were founded by three virgin saints, Craeb, Find, and Lassar, who were the daughters of Ere, son of Larr of the Dal Messin-Corb of Leinster (who were one of the four chief families in Leinster). It was said they 'had a church at Cill-na-nlngean, Killininny, near Tallaght, where they were venerated, October 26.' Four other virgin saints, styled 'daughters of Mac laar', were connected with Kilmainham – Darinell, Cael, Darbelin, and Conngheall; they were relatives of the saints at Killininny, and they also had a connection with the church there.

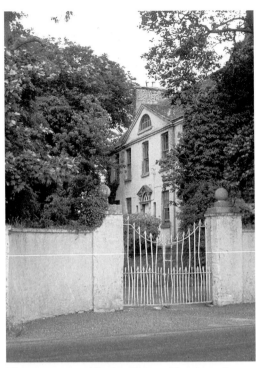

The entrance to Allenton House. (Courtesy of South County Dublin Library)

Mr Timothy Muldoon, a well-known farmer and horse breeder, owned Allenton for many years and when he died his nephew Mr Kirby became the owner of the house. He began to demolish it on New Year's Day 1983 but members of the local An Taisce Heritage Committee and of Tallaght Historical Society (especially Mrs Margaret Taylor) obtained a court injunction against Mr Kirby to stop the demolition. However, Allenton was further damaged by fire and was finally demolished entirely in August 1984.

10

TYMON LODGE

The football pitch at Scoil Treasa in Firhouse was once the location of Tymon Lodge. The tree-lined avenue that led to the lodge is still there, between Carrigwood Estate and the Firhouse road. The building itself was demolished in the 1970s. The house was built in the time of Queen Anne (1702–1714).

Tymon Lodge was an old-fashioned house with a curious chimney stack, a moat and a walled garden with a stream which supplied an ancient bath house, about 30ft by 12ft. The house could only be accessed by a drawbridge which appealed to George Moore's reclusive method of writing. 'No one could drop in while I am working,' he said.

George Moore (1852–1933) was a novelist. He came from a Roman Catholic landed family who lived at Moore Hall in County Mayo. He moved to Paris to study art in the 1870s and while there had his first book published in 1877. The Moore family were considered fair landlords and had a tradition of not evicting tenants and refusing to carry firearms when travelling round the estate.

Moore moved back to Ireland to pursue his interest in the Gaelic language revival and his ambition to establish the Irish Literary Theatre. He visited the lodge with the intention of renting it while he stayed in Dublin in 1886, and described it in a letter he wrote to his future mistress 'Stella', an English painter whose real name was Clara Christian (1868–1906):

> My dear Stella, the question is can I live in Ireland without you? And I besought her for the sake of her art. The Irish Mountains are as beautiful as the Welsh. Dublin is backed by blue hills, and you won't be obliged to live in a detestable cottage as you were last year in Wales, but in a fine house. And I told her that in my search for one to live in I had come across a house in Clondalkin, or near it, that would suit her perfectly – a moated stead built in the time of Anne, and seeing she was interested, I described how I crossed the moat by a little bridge, and between the bridge and the front door there were about thirty yards of gravel. The left wall rises sheer out of the moat: on the other side there is a pathway, and at the back a fairly large garden – close on a hundred yards, I should say – and you like gardening, Stella.
>
> I'm afraid that so much stagnant water [*sic*].
>
> But dear one, the water of the moat is not stagnant; it is fed at the upper end by a stream, and it trickles away by the bridge to the brook.

And the house itself?

It is two-storied and there are some fine rooms in it, one that I think you could paint in. My recollection is a little dim, but I remember a dining room and a very handsome drawing room, and I think my impression was a thousand pounds spent upon it would give you such a house, as you couldn't get anywhere else. Of that I'm sure, and the country about it is all your art requires. I remember a row of fine chestnuts, and beyond it a far reaching stretch of tilth to the river Liffey. Promise me that you'll come?

Stella became George Moore's mistress in 1899 and followed him to Tymon Lodge in 1901, impressed by his eccentricities and impulsiveness. But she ended the relationship in 1904, and on 11 January 1905 she married Charles McCarthy, the City Architect of Dublin.

She retained Tymon Lodge as her home after her marriage and died there in childbirth in 1906. Before her death she presented the Hugh Lane's Gallery with her painting 'Meditations'.

The artist Dame Ethel Walker (1861–1951) was a close friend of Clara Christian in the 1880s and the two women lived, studied, and worked together as fellow artists before Clara moved to Dublin.

11

DOLLYMOUNT (McCARTHY'S CASTLE)

Montpelier House, or Dollymount as it was originally named, is also known as McCarthy's Castle. Its ruins, at the foot of Montpelier Hill, can still be seen today, including the arms of the Earls of Ely, cut into the stone over the hall door. The name Dollymount suggests that it was intended for the occupation of the lovely Dolly Monroe.

The house was built by Lord Henry Earl of Ely at the end of the eighteenth century. The two-storey building had an impressive north-east-facing frontage with arched entrances and bow windows. The rooms were lofty and well proportioned, with marble chimneypieces and beautifully stuccoed ceilings. The windows commanded a lovely view of County Dublin, with its countless villas, and of the city overhung with a smoky cloud. Beyond it gleamed the bright waters of Dublin Bay; and off in the distance lay Howth, Ireland's Eye, Lambay, and the coastline a glorious prospect on a fine clear day.

On each side of the house were large arched gateways, surmounted by stone balls. On the sides of each of the gateways were long wings, containing servants' apartments and stables. At each end stood a square three-storey tower, with castellated walls and Gothic windows. The whole front was about 120 yards in length. Behind the house were extensive out-offices, kennels, barns, haggard, and all the requirements of a great hunting establishment. From the back entrance a paved road once went up the hill towards Piperstown.

Lord Henry, Earl of Ely's first wife was Frances Monroe, probably the aunt of Dolores 'Dolly' Monroe, who was a celebrated beauty in whose honour the house was named. A contemporary writer said:

Her stature was majestic, and her air and demeanour were nature itself. The peculiar splendour of her carriage was softened by the most affable condescension; and as sensibility gave lustre to her eye, so discretion gave security to her heart; and while her charms inspired universal rapture, the authority of her innocence regulated and restrained. The softest roses that ever youth and modesty poured out on beauty glowed on the lips of Dorothea. Never did beauty appear so amiable a virtue, so adorned as in this incomparable virgin.

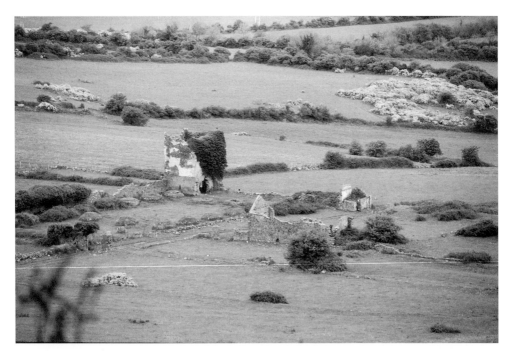

Dollymount in ruin, 1997. (Courtesy of South County Dublin Library)

After this paragon, this place was called Dollymount, which name it bore for many years.

Lord Ely frequently rode up from his castle at Rathfarnham. When supervising the planting of trees on the grounds at Dollymount one day he told the men, 'If I live until these trees are large enough to make a coffin for me; I will make gentlemen of you all; but I am going to do an act that Ireland will ever rue.' He alluded to his signing the petition for the Act of Union.

The Ely's were absentees and the building soon fell into ruin so too did Rathfarnham Castle. Dollymount suffered mainly at the hands of a tenant called Jack Kelly who wrecked the house to ensure his tenancy would not be disturbed. The house would have survived unattended but Kelly felled the trees and sold them, stripped lead from the roof and used the wood in the house for firewood. The marble slabs of the chimney pieces were used as thresholds and lintels in piggeries. All, except for the tower at the western end, was eventually demolished in 1950.

12

DILLON'S HUNTING LODGE

Dillon Lodge or Ballinascorney House was pleasantly situated in the shelter of its woods, over which rises what is locally known as 'The Black Hill'. Built in the eighteenth century as a hunting lodge by the Dillons of Belgard, it was first known as Dillon Lodge. It then stood in the middle of a deer park of about 80 acres.

At the end of the eighteenth century it was occupied by the Bagnal family and it was to here that Robert Emmet and his party first fled after the failure of their rebellion in 1803 (see chapter 18).

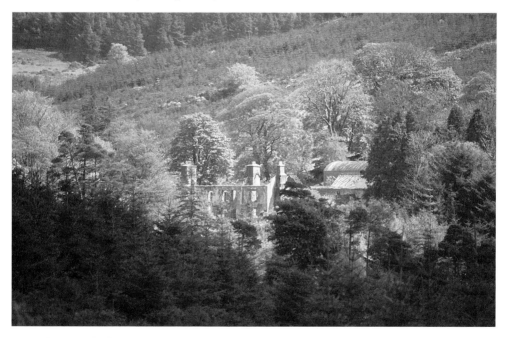

The ruin of Dillon's Hunting Lodge/Ballinascorney House. (Courtesy of South County Dublin Library)

The next owner of the lodge was Gerald Tench, who held the post of registrar in the Four Courts. Tench lived at Dillon's Lodge part of each year for many years after his retirement, about 1852, from his office in the Four Courts. He had risen from a very humble post to a very lucrative one. He was paralysed and drove everywhere in a four-wheeled carriage. In the house he had a wheelchair, in which he rolled himself where he wished. After his death a steward of his, named Ward, lived in the lodge until it was leased to Major Knox, proprietor of *The Irish Times*. Knox lived in great style here. Nearly every week in the season he drove his well-appointed four-horse drag, filled with ladies and gentlemen, to his mountain home, and there entertained them royally. He organised a band of twenty or thirty performers from the staff at *The Irish Times*. He dressed these in uniform, and had a large omnibus, in which they were frequently driven up to the lodge to play for the guests. The music could be heard for miles around, as they played their drums, trumpets, and fifes on the top of the bus, on their way up and down, creating great excitement among the locals, until the novelty wore off. Poor Major Knox overworked himself. He died too soon. Had he lived, he would have had a great career.

Mr Joseph McGrath, one of the pioneers of the Irish Hospitals' Trust, lived here for a period, as did Dr O'Rahilly of the well-known O'Rahilly family. Like Cobbe's Lodge it was often used as a headquarters by the rebels during the troubled years.

The house was destroyed by fire in 1987 and only a ruin remains.

13

FRIARSTOWN HOUSE

At one time the Franciscan Friars owned the land in this area and this is how the place became known as Friarstown. Behind Bohernabreena chapel, on the road known as Fox Hill, is the entrance to Friarstown House, once the residence of Ponsonby Shaw (1784–1871), brother of Sir Robert Shaw, of Bushy Park, Terenure.

Shaw spent a great deal of money on improvements at Friarstown, reclaiming and planting the grounds, which he converted into a pretty wooded glen, with winding walks, grottoes and miniature waterfalls. At the head of the glen he formed a lake by damming the course of the stream, but it was only just finished when it burst and swept all before it, wrecking his work. He was so disheartened by this mishap that he made no attempt to repair the damage.

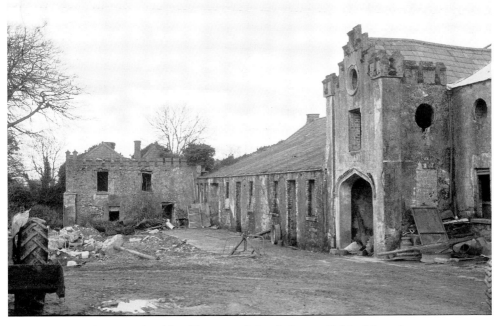

Friarstown house and stables. (Courtesy of South County Dublin Library)

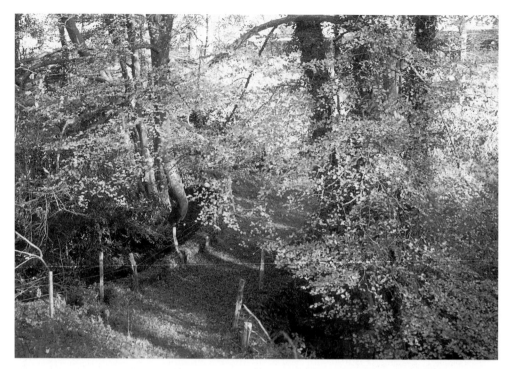

Friarstown glen. (Courtesy of South County Dublin Library)

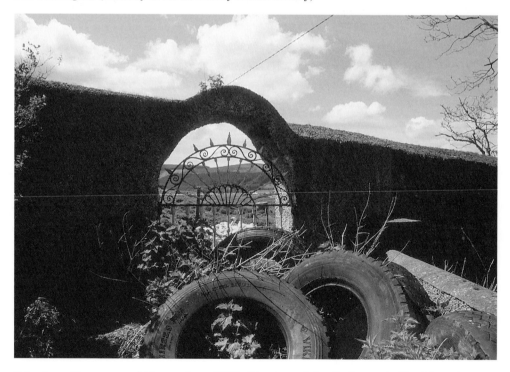

Friarstown House wrought-iron gate, *c*. 2004. (Courtesy of South County Dublin Library)

It was not repaired for many years, until a Captain Bayley took the place and rebuilt it. A Scotchman named Watson succeeded him; but as he wasn't interested in the ornamental aspect of the garden and it fell into neglect once again.

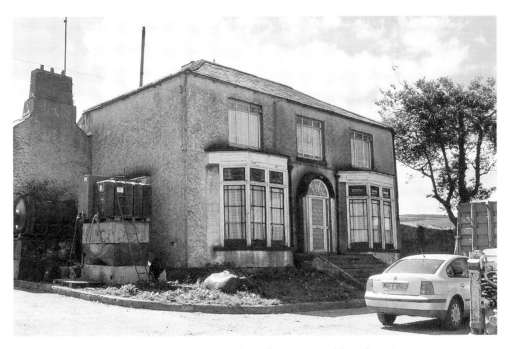

Friarstown House, *c.* 2004. (Courtesy of South County Dublin Library)

14

ANN MOUNT

Ann Mount, near Glassamucky, was once a monastery connected with the Carmelite Order at Clondalkin. It was founded in 1821 by Brother Maurice Collins and John Steward, who were distressed at the lack of education among the children of the locality. They leased these premises from Charles Cobbe, the landowner, and, with a few other brothers, set about establishing the monastery and school. These brothers got no help from the Board of Education but had to depend on voluntary contributions to keep the school open.

The monastery consisted of a range of thatched buildings around an enclosed yard and included the dwelling place of the monks, the schoolhouse, an oratory where Mass was celebrated every Sunday and a guesthouse. On each pier of the

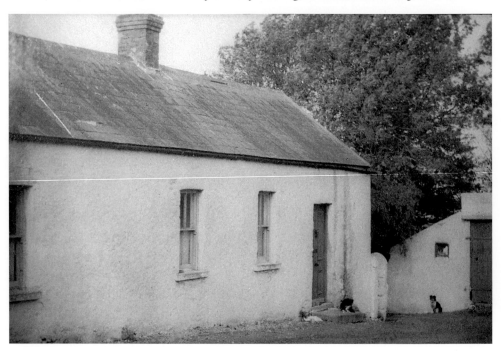

Ann Mount. (Courtesy of South County Dublin Library)

entrance gate was a stone cross. According to the law at that time, the prior had to become the proprietor of the premises as a religious community was not allowed to hold property. Collins, who was described as the prior, died in 1865 at the ripe old age of 94 years and his place was taken by John Stewart.

About this time a social society known as St Ann's Club used to meet here for dinner on Sundays and spend the fine evenings playing quoits and other games. According to a contemporary writer, many of its members were more famous for their musical, facetious or gastronomic achievements than for their athletic endeavours. The monks supplied the room, fuel, and water, and many a pleasant evening was spent in the pure air of the mountains. A fixture card for the year 1872 lists among the members: J.F. Lombard, S.S. Waterhouse, M.H. Chamberlaine, T. Fry, H.J. Tyrell, J. Ireland, B. Elliott, M. Brooks, T. Nedley, T. Cranfield and G.J. Alexander, all names that were well known in the professional and commercial life of the city.

John Stewart died in 1887. By then there were only a few brothers left and little effort was made to continue the community life. Although a new pavilion had been built, the school was closed. The building was later used as a barn. A disastrous fire damaged the oratory and other buildings and from 1891 the chapel was no longer used. Brother Kearns was the last survivor of this pioneering group and he continued to occupy the premises and work the farm. He eventually married Sarah Williams and in 1895 the place passed to his widow. It passed to the O'Riordans in 1925.

The last phase of Ann Mount as a guesthouse has tended to eclipse its earlier history as an education centre, and with the passing of the older generation there will be little to remind the coming generations of the achievements of the Carmelite brothers. The social parties were well remembered (some of the prominent Gaelic League Revivalists were attracted to the valley and spent many nights socialising here) and so were the difficulties experienced in getting the carriages up and down the steep hill at Friarstown and the way they used to throw down coppers to the scrambling children.

The monument in St Anne's (St Sanctan's) graveyard (which has a reputation for being Ireland's oldest graveyard and dates back to Druidical times), to those who know of its existence, will ever stand as a reminder of the monks:

Erected by a few friends as a token of respect to Maurice Collins
For 44 years Prior of St. Anne's Monastery
who died 31st Jan 1865 aged 94 years
and his religious
Andrew McGuirk died 13 Nov 1842 aged 46 years
John Farrell died 27th Jan 1854 aged 67 years
Patrick McGuirk died 16th Oct aged 69 years
Mathew Kelly died 22 June 1873 aged 68 years
John Stewart died 17th April 1887 aged 93 years
For 16 years Prior of St. Anne's.

15

ST ANNE'S CHURCH

St Anne's was built on the site of an older church that had become too old and inadequate to cater for the growing population. The foundation stone of the new building was laid in 1868 by one of the most distinguished Irish churchmen of his time, his Eminence Cardinal Cullen who had been archbishop of Dublin prior to his appointment as the first Irish cardinal in 1866. The church was blessed on 14 August 1870 and the ceremony was performed by the Most Revd Dr Moran Lord Bishop of Grahamstown, South Africa and Fr Tom Burke, a Dominican known as the 'Prince of Preachers' who, it was reported, gave one of his best sermons on

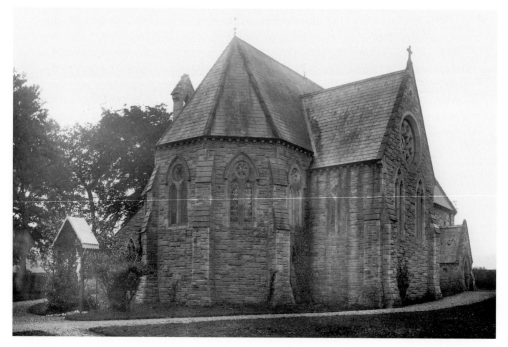

An old picture of St Anne's Roman Catholic church. Note the position of the free-standing crucifix, which now stands against the wall of the church. (Courtesy of South County Dublin Library)

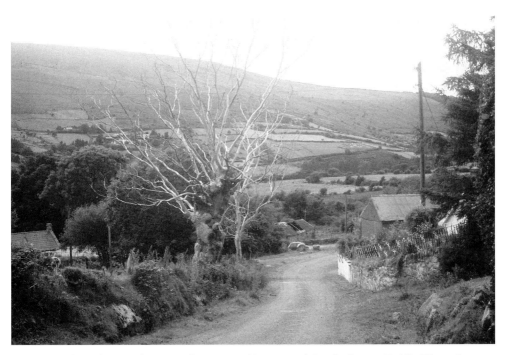

Cunard in Glenasmole near Kilnasantan. (Courtesy of South County Dublin Library)

the occasion. In fact the Dominicans were an integral part of life in Bohernabreena. St Anne's first curate was Fr E. Buckley.

The well-known architect J.J. McCarthy (also responsible for many prominent churches such as Mount Argus at Harold's Cross) designed the church so it would merge with the natural beauty of the setting. The design is thirteenth-century French Gothic style. The exterior stone used in the building is granite, which was cut and dressed on the Glassamucky Mountain between Cunard and the Featherbed. All the work was carried out voluntarily by the parishioners. The stained-glass window behind Our Lady's altar shows the Blessed Virgin on one side holding the infant Jesus, and on the opposite side stands St Joseph. The holy water fonts in the church entrance are reputed to have been from the original old church, thus keeping a link through the generations. Irish was still spoken in the valley down to the beginning of the twentieth century and it was reported that when the new chapel was opened the first sermon was preached in Irish because it was the language of the district.

The catchment area of the parish was large, from Newlands to Kippure. People walked from Kilinarden over Boothmans fields and down from the head of the valley in Glenasmole. They began walking at 7.30 for 8.30 mass and got home at about 10.30, without even a drink of water.

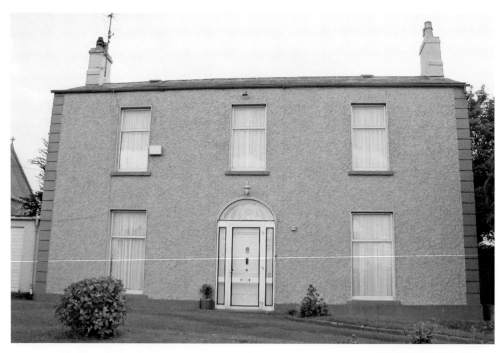

The parish priest's house in Bohernabreena. (Courtesy of South County Dublin Library)

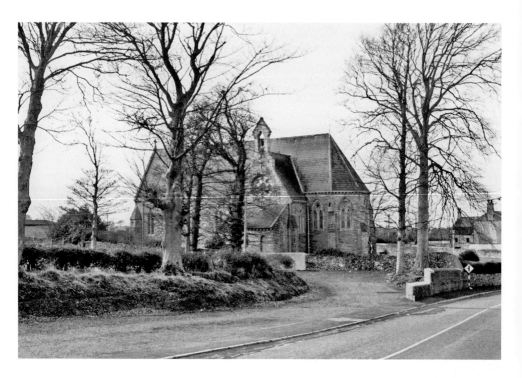

St Anne's in 1977. (Courtesy of South County Dublin Library)

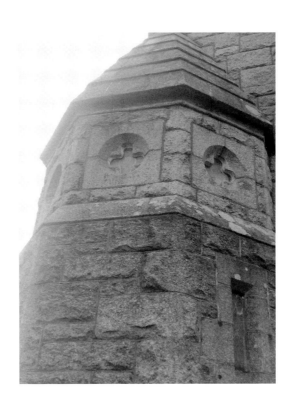

One of the angle buttresses with quatrefoil windows of St Anne's.

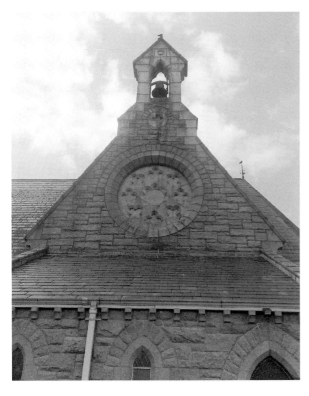

The wheel window below the bell tower of St Anne's.

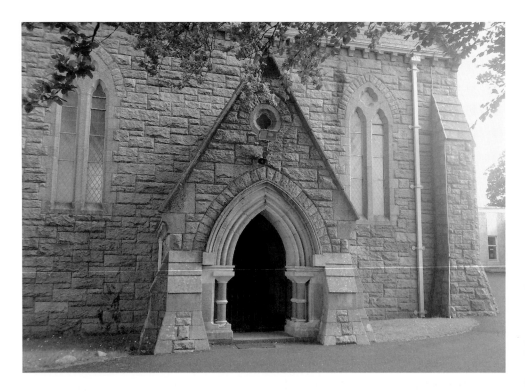

The gabled entrance porch with roll mouldings and paired colonnettes of St Anne's.

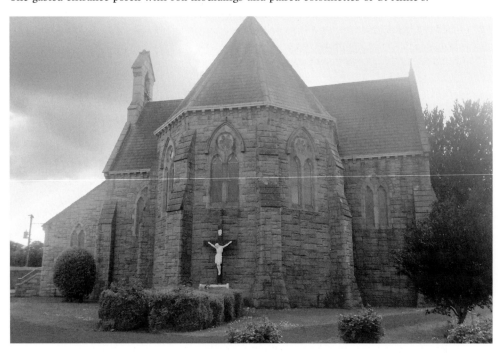

St Anne's presbytery today with the crucifix in its new position.

16

KILLAKEE HOUSE

Killakee House was built in the early nineteenth century. Although the exact date is not known, it is clearly marked on a map of the White Estate, dated 1806. No longer standing, Killakee House was a two-storied stucco-faced house of symmetrical aspect with a curved bow in the centre front and similar bows in the elevations. After the Norman invasion the estate of Killakee was granted to Walter de Ridleford. In the thirteenth century it passed to the Crown but was of no value due to the attacks of the Irish tribes. Killakee was later granted by Henry VIII to Sir Thomas Luttrell. During the seventeenth century these lands were forfeited by the Luttrells and granted to Dr Dudley Loftus. The population of Killakee was at that time recorded as twenty-one.

Early in the eighteenth century the estate passed to Speaker Connolly and later in that century to Mr Luke White, a millionaire Dublin bookseller, who originally owned the house. He also owned Luttrellstown Estate in Lucan. He died in London in February 1924 and the property passed to his second son, Colonel Samuel White of the county militia, who was a Member of Parliament for County Leitrim. Colonel White

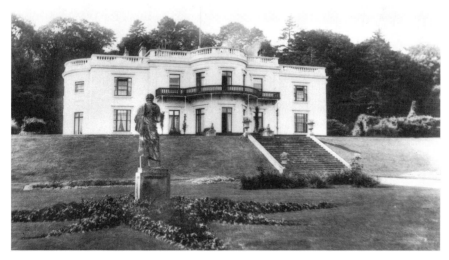

Killakee House, a magnificent house that must have been an incredible sight at the time it was built, was sadly demolished in 1941. (Courtesy of South County Dublin Library)

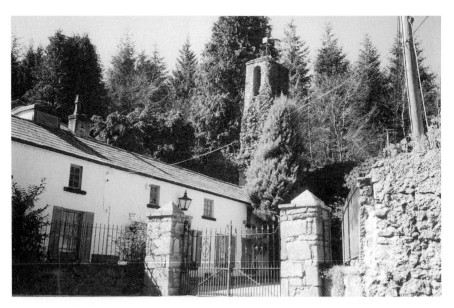

The Steward's House or Dower House at Killakee.

lived at Killakee in considerable style. He owned 2,900 acres there, half of which was let out to tenants. The gardens were spectacularly landscaped and contained many exotic plants, some of which were kept in large glasshouses. Terraced lawns were laid out with shrubs and trees and a large fountain graced the front lawn.

The estate descended through the female line to Lord Massey, who married Colonel White's youngest sister. Lord Massey was descended from Hugh Massey who came to Ireland in 1641 to suppress the rebellion and held lands at Duntrileague, County Limerick, as well as at Caher and Mitchelstown.

The last Lord Massey to live here was Hugh Hamon Charles George, 8th Baron Massey. He was declared bankrupt in 1924 and was evicted from his house; the contents of the house were auctioned. Being ill with paralysis at the time, he was carried out on a stretcher while the bailiffs looked on. He was allowed, however, to occupy one of his own gate lodges, Beehive Cottage, where he resided with his wife and son until his death in 1958. He seldom visited the city but occupied his time looking after the cottage, while his wife worked in the Hospitals Sweep Office. He spent much time collecting fuel from his own woods, which he transported in a small hand cart.

Killakee House was demolished in 1941 and the estate was taken over by the land commission.

Within the estate (known as Massey's Wood) are many magnificent trees and rivulets cascading down through rocky gorges. There is a fine avenue of monkey-puzzle trees that leads to the site of the house. Walled gardens mark the site of the orchards and used to shelter the glasshouses that once stood there, and beside the stream are ruins of a watermill that was used to power a sawmill. Within this forest are some of the finest woodland paths in the country.

On a summit over the stream are the remains of a wedge tomb dating from the late Stone Age (about 4,000 years ago). This consists of an enclosed chamber built of large flat stones with an entrance facing the west.

17

DOWER HOUSE

The Steward's House, as it was originally known, was a hunting lodge built around 1765 by the Conolly family. It was later used as a dower house by the Massey family and as a residence for the manager of the estate. The belfry at the rear, which was added later, was used to call workers in for meals.

In 1968, Margaret and Nicholas O'Brien bought Dower House on Killakee road, a dilapidated building that they planned to renovate and turn into an arts centre.

During the renovations, some of the workers, who lived on the property, grew used to ghostly sounds and eerie occurrences. But one day, a large black cat appeared and then as suddenly as it appeared, it vanished. The workmen were unsettled as there was a legend about the phantom cat in the area, but Margaret attributed the men's stories to their imagination. However, she finally saw the creature and she too became a believer. The first time she saw the black feline,

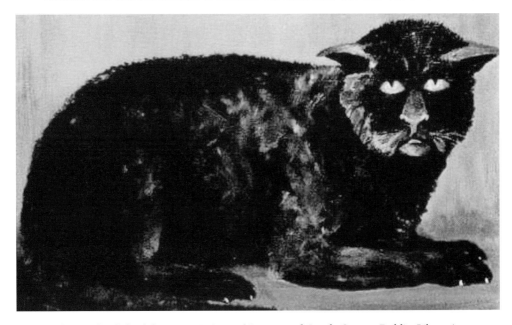

'The Black Cat of Killakee', by Tom McAssey. (Courtesy of South County Dublin Library)

which she claimed was the size of a Dalmatian, it was sitting on the hallway flagstone floor, glaring at her. Every door in the house had been locked prior to and after the phantom announced its presence and suddenly vanished.

On another occasion, artist Tom McAssey and two other men were working in a room when the temperature dropped drastically. Suddenly the door swung open and a hazy form came into view. Thinking it was someone playing a joke, McAssey called out to see who was there and told the prankster he could be seen, although they couldn't see anyone, or anything. The three men momentarily froze in horror when the response was not human; it was a menacing snarl. Then, they saw the figure of a growling black feline with eyes glowing red and beside it a shadowy figure growled, 'You cannot see me. You don't even know who I am!'

Mrs O'Brien had an exorcism performed which apparently got rid of the fearsome feline.

McAssey painted a picture of the cat. The face seems to be humanoid and eerie: this could be the way the features actually appeared, what McAssey thought he saw or a stylised version of the head.

In the early part of the twentieth century, Tower Hall (as it was known for a time) was visited regularly by George Russell (Æ), George Moore, W.B. Yeats and Katherine Tynan. Countess Markievicz recommended the house to men on the run from British forces, because its unexpected stairways, leading to convenient exits, made it an ideal hideaway.

In 1971 a plumber working on the house discovered the skeletal remains of what has been described as a 'dwarfish figure'. Local superstition associates this with a tale linked to the Hellfire Club in which a dwarf was drowned in a barrel. For many years the building operated as an art centre and craft shop, then as a restaurant. Tom McAssey's painting 'The Black Cat of Killakee' was hung in the dining area for all to see. The stories were published in the national papers and caused quite a stir, creating a lot of publicity. The restaurant eventually closed in 2000 and the house has been privately owned since.

18

ROBERT EMMET'S VISIT

After the failed rising of 1803 Robert Emmet and his men left Dublin City disguised as French soldiers. They retreated to Butterfield Lane, and very early on Sunday 24 July, most of them went to the house of Brien Devlin, who lived close by. He was the father of Anne Devlin. They spent the day there without seeming depressed by their recent failure; they did not mention the rising or their future plans. On Monday Mrs Devlin was getting some milk churned and some of them volunteered to lend a hand when a woman raised the latch of the door and walked in without knocking. She gazed about her with an apparent air of stupidity, made an excuse for coming in, and left. She was the wife of a yeoman.

Mr Grierson, the King's Printer, had a residence near there and the woman went and told him how she had seen fifty French officers at Devlin's. Mr Grierson had just sat down to dinner with a couple of friends and he asked them if he should go to Rathfarnham Castle to report the news. The wine was flowing, the night was young, and, being in such a remote place Grierson felt secure from any attack. It was decided there was no need to stir till later that night.

The butler, while passing through the hall, heard the woman's story of the French officers. A supporter of the rebels, he knew Arthur Devlin well and lost no time in getting the word out to Brian Devlin that their whereabouts was known. As soon as it became dark Devlin had horses ready for them, and a veteran of 1798 named Cummins, undertook to guide them to John Doyle's of Ballymeece.

They arrived at two o'clock on 26 July. John Doyle, a farmer, was asleep in bed after drinking heavily that night and woke to a room of men dressed in French military uniforms complete with plumed hats. The following is taken from his court testimony.

They desired me to take some spirits, which I refused. They then lifted me over into the middle of the bed, and I gave them no assistance – they lay down two of them, one upon each side of me. One of them said, 'I had a French General and a French Colonel beside me, what I never had before'. Which was true enough, I never had – I lay there between them for some hours, but between sleep and awake – when I was awake, I found them asleep and then I fell a listening, and I got up and stole out of bed, and I found some blunderbusses and a gun and some pistols.

The number of guns he believed was equal to the number of persons, who, on being collected at breakfast, amounted to fourteen. He identified the prisoner Robert Emmet as one of those who were in the bed with him.

Between eight and nine the following evening they left with their arms and went up the hill. They arrived at Rose Bagnal's house (Ballinascorney House) between eleven and twelve that night. The alarmed householders were treated with the greatest courtesy by the party, and suffered no further injury than the consumption of the contents of their pantry. Rose Bagnal was called to give evidence at Emmet's trial. In her deposition she claimed to have been so frightened she could not distinguish their uniforms, but said they wore green jackets with yellow and said that one of them was called a general but she could not identify any of them. On the night of Wednesday 27th, at nine o'clock, they moved on, declaring that they would not be the cause of any person suffering on their account.

They sheltered in a small glen not far from the Bagnals where the sky was the canvas of their tents and their only light was the stars in the heavens.

Here, chilled from the night air and morning dew, and no doubt suffering from want of food, on the morning of the 28th they made their way to Kearney's public house at Bohernabreena, about 2½ miles from the place where they had spent the night. The pub was first licensed in 1750 and in the early 1800s it was designated as a daily dispatch and collection point for the Royal Mail Coach. Kearney's (now the site of the Old Mill Pub and formerly Bridget Burke's Pub) was kept by William Kearney.

After eating and drinking they stayed on for a while, enjoying Kearney's home-brewed mountain dew when John Robinson, the barony constable of Upper Cross, who had spent the morning trying to pick up their trail, stepped into Kearney's amongst them. He certainly did not expect to meet them there, and he was near paying a large price for his morning visit but for William Kearney, who discreetly told him he wasn't welcome and saw him away from danger.

In Kearney's house there was a small upper room with a very narrow staircase leading to it. It had scarcely the appearance of an apartment used for ordinary purposes. It was a cockloft and had no windows but did have a skylight. The men gathered there still in uniform as they had no other clothes. About eleven o'clock, as one of the men was looking out through the skylight, he saw a military party, composed of army and yeomen, something more than 600 strong. They were commanded by Mr La Touche, Captain of the Rathfarnham Mounted Corps of Yeomen, and Mr Ponsonby Shaw as second-in-command. They were returning from Mrs Bagnal's, where they had been searching for the rebels.

By the time the rebels had spotted the soldiers they were too late for them to make an attempt at escape; they would either have to surrender or stand and fight. The officers formed a cordon about the house but a good distance from it. The house was slated and had fairly good walls, but they were very low and there were no windows out of which they could fire. There were only twelve of them in the attic. The odds were against them but they resolved they wouldn't be taken alive.

Arthur Devlin knelt down in the middle of the floor, with the muzzle of his blunderbuss covering the head of the narrow stairs, his left hand steadily supporting the piece, and his finger on the trigger. All was now as silent as death. Kearney and his wife stood on the floor below, in silence. Mr La Touche and Mr Shaw entered and some of their men drew a little closer to the house.

Mr Shaw said, 'Well, Kearney, have you got any strangers here?'

'No, Sir,' was the reply. 'The house is not large, and you can easily see through it.'

Mr Shaw looked into a taproom whose door was partly open, and then, throwing a look all round, he saw the narrow stairs leading to the apartment where the very men he was searching for lay crouched on the floor, ready to fire. Just before Shaw entered Kearney saw some baskets at the door, which were used for bringing turf down from the mountains across a horse's back. These he grabbed quickly and threw on the steps of the stairs in a careless and disorderly manner, to give that passage the appearance of not being in use. Mr Shaw, pointing upwards, asked if there was anyone up there.

'No, Sir,' said Kearney, firmly. 'We make no use of that place but to throw some light lumber on it; it's not able to bear any weight.'

Shaw had one foot on the first step and was rising to the second when Mrs Kearney caught the edge of his coat, and, with a gentle jerk, said, 'Oh, Sir, if you go up there you will fall down through it and be killed.'

Little did he know, if he had taken another step he would really have been killed; he would have received Devlin's fire through the head. Shaw and La Touche left with their men and a little later, when the coast was clear, Emmet and the rest of the men left too and headed back to Ballinascorney House. Without doubt it was to Kearney and his family that Shaw owed his life.

On that same evening, Anne Devlin and her friend Miss Wyld took a jaunting car and drove out to the rebels with some letters. They were sitting on a sunny bank at Mrs Bagnal's when the two young women approached them. A council had been held, and it was decided that each man should do the best he could for himself. Emmet divided what money he had between them and he got into the jaunting car with Devlin and Wyld. After a moving farewell they drove off in the direction of Dublin before he parted with them a little outside of Rathfarnham.

Robert Emmet was arrested a month later, on 25 August, at Harold's Cross.

19

EXECUTION OF
THE KEARNEYS

Hangings in Dublin were very common occurrences; in the eighteenth century there were more people hung in Britain and Ireland than in the rest of Europe. It was in the field on Kiltipper Road, close to the Old Bawn bridge (opposite the Aylesbury estate), that the Kearneys were hanged in 1816. These three men, a father and two sons, Peter, Joe and Billy (William) Kearney, were convicted of conspiracy to murder John Kinlan of Friarstown, an employee of Ponsonby Shaw.

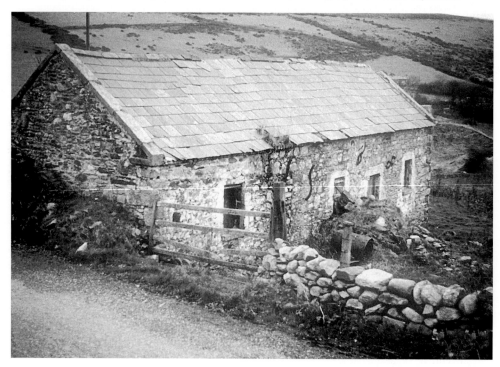

The Kearneys' cottage at Piperstown. (Courtesy of South County Dublin Library)

The Kearneys, who lived in Piperstown, had been heard to say that they would finish Kinlan whenever they got the chance and when Kinlan disappeared one night after a shot had been heard, they immediately came under suspicion. Kinlan's body could not be found but a hatchet was located near the Kearneys' house with blood on it and hair that resembled Kinlan's. This circumstantial evidence was enough to secure the death penalty.

The Kearneys were escorted from Kilmainham by a troop of Dragoons to the field where three gallows had been erected. On the way they passed Bushy Park, where the Shaw family lived, and requested that their carriage halted. The Kearneys knelt and cursed the Shaw family for all eternity.

Thousands of people had assembled to witness the execution and their sympathy would appear to have been all on the side of the convicted men. One son climbed up the ladder and helped his father up, followed by the second son. Another brother, who was not accused of the crime, offered to take his father's place, but his request was refused.

The rope for William Kearney, who was very tall, was too long and when he dropped his feet touched the ground. The executioner had to dig a hole beneath William's feet as he dangled from the noose. When the hole was deep enough the hangman had to pull down on William's legs below the knees to finish the job. His mother, understandably, had to be held back by soldiers as she tried to attack the hangman.

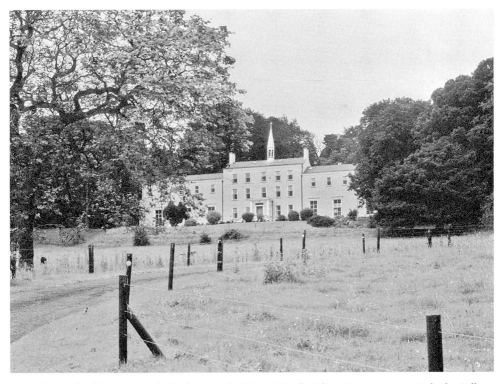

Originally Footmount, built by Lundy Foot, this building is now now Orlagh College. (Courtesy of South County Dublin Library)

When the men were dead, their bodies were cut down, thrown into a cart, covered with lime sacks from a lime kiln which stood close by, and brought back to Kilmainham Jail where they were buried. Many years later three skeletons, which were said to be their remains, were exhumed at Kilmainham.

When the gallows were being removed, they nearly fell on the hangman, Thomas Galvin (who also executed Robert Emmet), and suddenly the sombre atmosphere turned to one of raucous laughter.

The judge who convicted the three men was Lundy Foot. He was very unpopular in the area as he was renowned for cruel and harsh sentences. Foot came from an extremely wealthy family who were well known for snuff and tobacco manufacture. He lived in a house now called Orlagh House (then called Footmount) which is now currently owned by the Augustinian order. Following the hanging the judge feared for his life and moved to County Kilkenny where he was shot, but although wounded badly he recovered. He was eventually murdered in 1835, beaten to death with a stone, at Rosbercon, New Ross. It was believed that Foot's murder was a revenge killing for his role in the execution of the Kearneys.

20

THE RIVER DODDER

The River Dodder rises in the Dublin Mountains, which separate South County Dublin from Wicklow. Some of its waters, however, are drawn from lands lying near the summits of mountains in the County of Wicklow. The source of the Liffey is no more than 4 miles from that of the Dodder, so that they begin and end together, though widely separated in most places. There are four principal streams which come together to form the Dodder. The first is Tromanallison (Allison's Brook); the next is the largest, Moreen's Brook (the supposed site of Dá Derga's Hostel), rising on the north-eastern slope of Kippure at the back of Lough Bray at 2,473ft. This runs down a steep valley, bounded on either side by lofty and precipitous hills, covered with boulders, gravel and clay. It passes Heathfield Lodge and flows on to Castle Kelly near where it is joined by the third stream, Cot Brook, and then Slade Brook before it enters the reservoir.

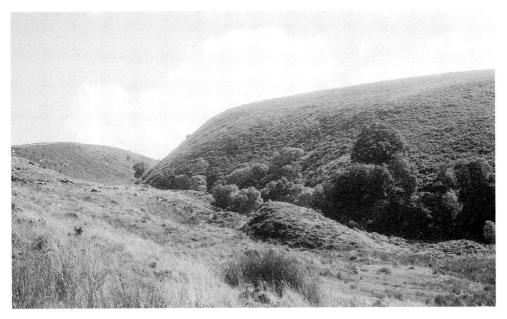

The source of the Dodder in the Glenasmole Valley. (Courtesy of South County Dublin Library)

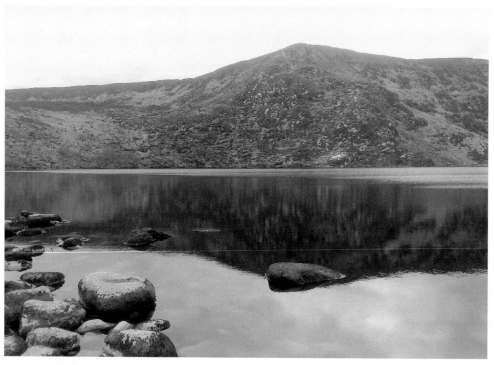

Lough Bray, near the source of Moreen's Brook.

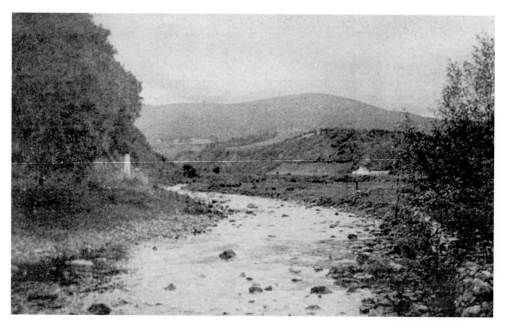

The Dodder at Glenasmole, taken in 1921 from the Fort Bridge Bohernabreena. (Courtesy of South County Dublin Library)

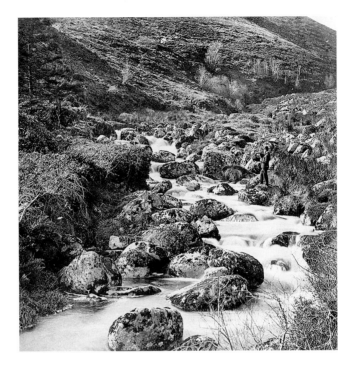

The Dodder at Glenasmole, *c.* 1880. (Courtesy of South County Dublin Library)

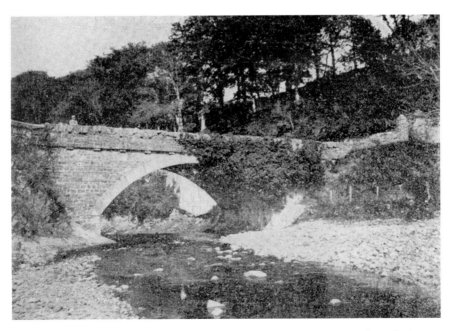

The Fort Bridge over the Dodder at Bohernabreena, *c.* 1895. (Courtesy of South County Dublin Library)

The Cataract of the Rowan Tree is a stream near the first cottage in Glenasmole. It flows in a narrow and twisting course through rocks and boulders, forming many a picturesque cascade and pool, and leaving the foot of St Mary's Cliff, where grew the giant ivy, celebrated in the Ossianic Poems, (recorded amongst the Ordnance Survey papers in the Royal Irish Academy). Sadly it grows no more. The river flows on under many a small rowan tree, no doubt lineal descendants of that which, in Oisín's time, bore berries larger than St Patrick's loaves. Lower down the Glenasmole Valley, the Dodder receives little streams from Glassmullaun, and one from the Holy Well of Kilnasantan, another at Ballymore Finn, and another at Allagour. Passing through Glassamucky, it reaches the end of the valley at Friarstown, or Bohernabreena. The river falls about 350ft in the first 2 miles, the banks being mostly formed of gravel and boulders.

THE MILLS ON THE DODDER

During the eighteenth century, many mills were located along the banks of the River Dodder. Most of the mills were outside the area of the valley, but the Dodder flows down through the valley and I have included this piece to show how much industry there once was so close to the picturesque valley. In fact, the Dodder was once one of Ireland's major industrial rivers. At the time the reservoir was built in Bohernabreena in the 1880s, there were forty-five mills along the Dodder of which fifteen were flour mills and the remainder were paper, paint, cardboard, cotton, saw, glue and dye mills, as well as distilleries, breweries, malt houses, foundries, tanneries, and a bacon-curing factory.

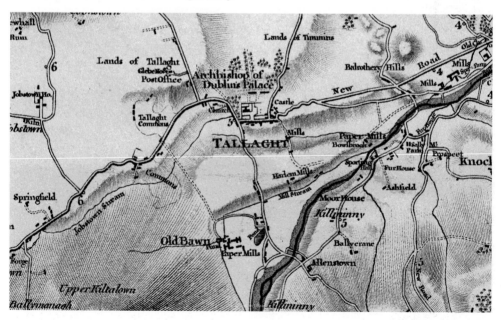

Taylor's 1816 map of Tallaght, showing the many mills in the area. (Courtesy of South County Dublin Library)

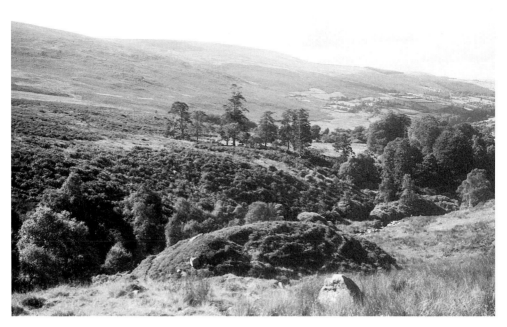

The view across the valley with the reservoir lake just visible on the right. (Courtesy of South County Dublin Library)

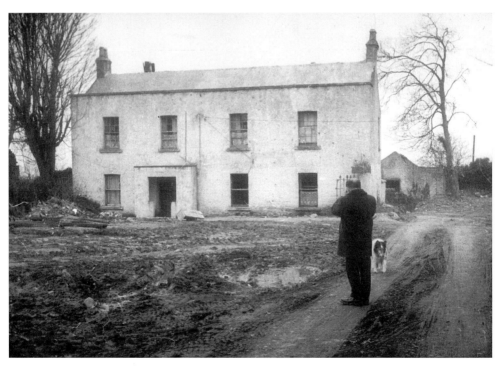

Haarlem Mills at Old Bawn. (Courtesy of South County Dublin Library)

At one time there was a small corn mill in Friarstown, worked by the Piperstown stream. It has long gone to decay. A little below Friarstown there was a parchment mill. Again, it is long gone. The water that supplied it must have been taken from the Ballinascorney stream.

At Old Bawn there was a paper mill, making newspapers. Next as the river runs were the Haarlem Mills in 1776, where previously the best bleaching green in Ireland was to be found (the bleached materials were left to dry on the ground, hence the name). Haarlem & Company were calico printers; in 1813 Mr Bewley was one of the principals. Next up there were four more mills, one of them being woollen and the others flour mills. The next mill was at Boldbrook and it made cardboard; then came the paper mills at Firhouse. There were other mills at Templeogue that ground flour.

The reservoir in Bohernabreena was constructed to supply the mills and it served Rathmines and Rathgar also. This was badly needed both for the mills and to have a source of clean drinking water, as there were so many mills that the waste water had polluted the Dodder to the extent that it had become poisonous; cattle and horses died from drinking it. Sometimes it was said to be the same colour as porter!

BOHERNABREENA RESERVOIR

The total catchment area (which is like a basin) of the Dodder is about 55 square miles, of which about 22 miles are hills and 32 are flat or of small incline. The river flows through a narrow cut in a natural embankment, extending across the end of the valley and the rapid floods, caused by the steepness of the sides of the catchment area, carried down great quantities of water. There were many attempts and large sums of money spent trying to prevent flooding along the Dodder over the years. Costly walls were built and then levelled by this powerful river. Bridges were swept away and new tracts of ground devastated. Over time the channel grew so deep that the river has become less volatile and less damage is done. But in times of very heavy rainfall the Dodder can still burst its banks and do a lot of damage, the most recent being during Hurricane Charley in 1986 when Ballsbridge was flooded.

The waters of Bohernabreena Reservoirs were trapped behind two dams built between 1883 and 1887 to provide for both Rathmines/Rathgar and the many mills that harnessed the power of the Dodder.

Shortly after it opened the reservoir became a favourite place to spend a day relaxing by the lakes. Whole families would arrive from the city and bring picnics during summer weekends and bank holidays. From the 1930s busses ran all day, ferrying people from the city out to the reservoir and back again. It became a very popular spot. This was known as 'going down the line' (the line being the road that runs through the waterworks by the lakes).

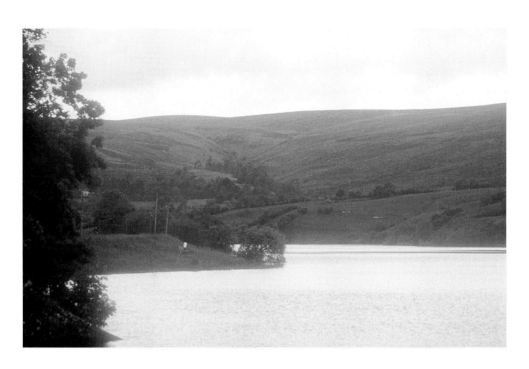

Bohernabreena Reservoir. (Courtesy of South County Dublin Library)

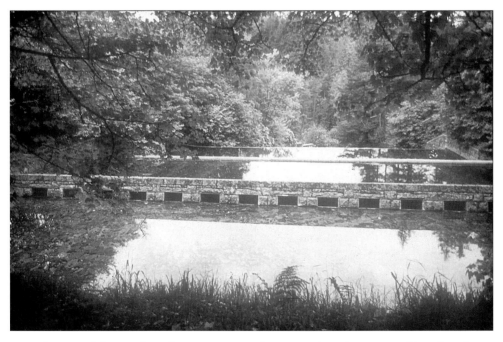

The upper lake at Bohernabreena Reservoir. (Courtesy of South County Dublin Library)

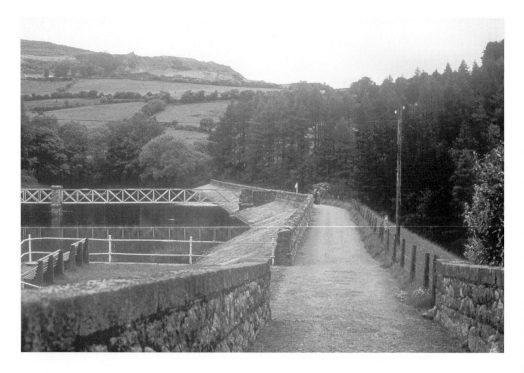

The lower lake with a walkway across the top of the dam and seats by the lakeside.

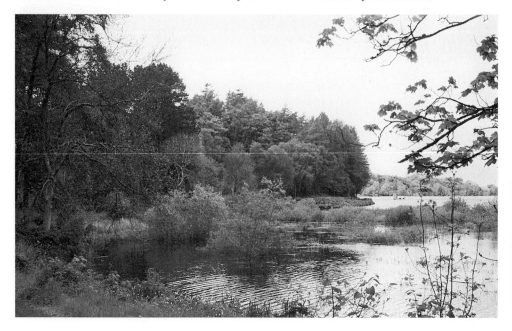

The lower lake in 1981 with the outlet tower and dam in the distance.

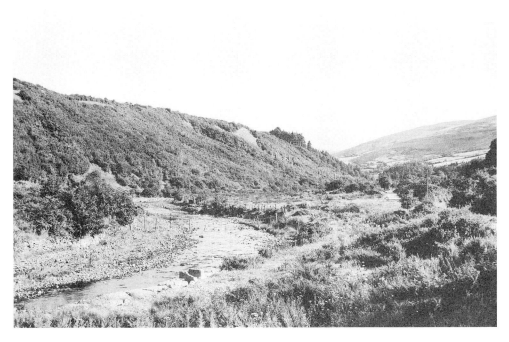

The Dodder flowing down from the first lake towards the reservoir entrance as it looked in the early 1900s.

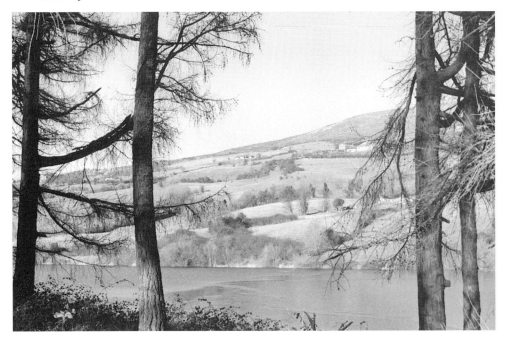

The lakes were a very popular place to go for a daytrip when the reservoir was first built.

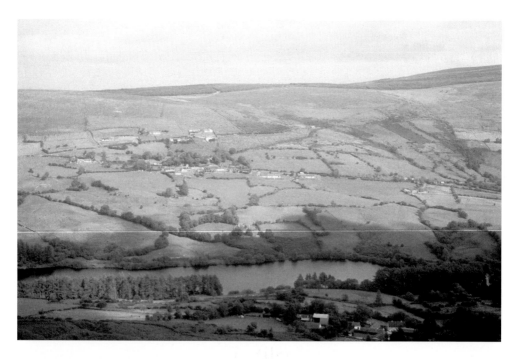

The view of Glassamucky and the upper lake from Ballymorefinn.

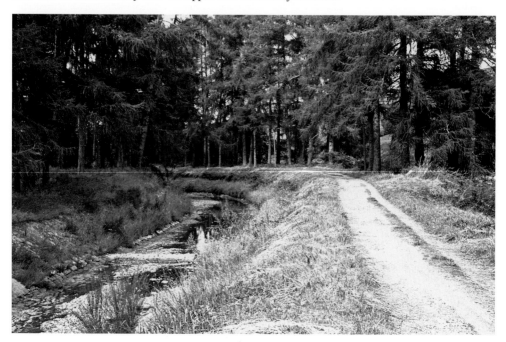

The pathway at the upper lake taken in the 1970s.

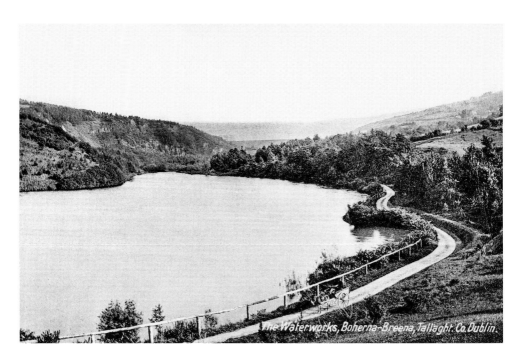

A postcard of Bohernabreena reservoir from 1945.

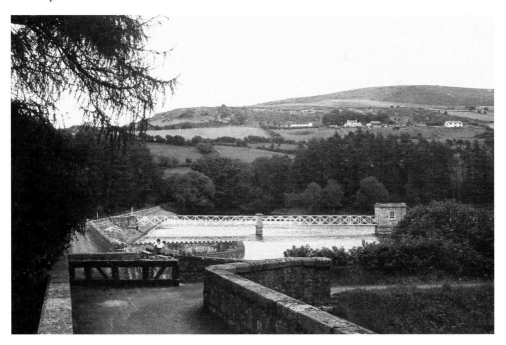

The spillway and outlet tower at the upper lake.

21

THE FAMINE YEARS

Malachi Horan from Killinarden published his memoirs and caused quite a stir in the literary world. So much so that Dr Douglas Hyde, the then President of Ireland, made a point of visiting the old man in his mountain retreat. Malachi wrote about life in the valley and spent much time there talking to locals and recording their stories. He mentions the Great Famine in his book *Malachi Horan Remembers* and attributes the survival of the people in the valley to their trading links with the city. In particular, 'It was the Indian meal that saved the people from being starved outright'. Dan Costelloe of Meath Street was the first to stock it and a poor man could buy it for three pence a day.

During the famine years the population decline in the valley wasn't particularly severe. The total recorded population of 863 in 1841 fell to 737 by 1851. This, for such a rural area, is quite unusual.

22

DE VALERA IN BALLINASCORNEY

This article from *The New York Times* caught my attention as it had a reference to Ballinascorney. On 7 July 1922 the Free State Army were trying to quell the revolution and capture Eamon De Valera. According to the report the Nationals were successful and, gaining ground, closed in on the rebels and pushed them back from Ballinascorney and Kilbride to Blessington. The report describes the rebels' outposts in the mountains as being very hard to find and states that some of the roads were blocked, trenches had been dug for ambush and mines had been laid. This made it very dangerous to search, but the Free State Troopers were closing in a wide circle and they were confident they would find the rebels or flush them out.

Though they didn't find De Valera, they did close in on an outpost and a gunfight ensued in Ballinascorney. The Free State Troopers won this round and twelve rebels were arrested.

There was another pitched battle on 8 July between the rebels and the Nationals at Brittas and Blessington along the tramline. The authorities were convinced that De Valera had left Ballinascorney and was now hiding out there. There were reported sightings of De Valera and Erskine Childers in the area. Harry Boland was hiding there too. In the report the Free State Troops held off even though they had the outpost surrounded; fearing there could be a blood bath they backed down. The rebels abandoned their outpost at Kilbride camp at this stage and everyone was retreating to Blessington, where it is reported there were over 500 insurgents.

By this stage, the Civil War was almost over and everything was getting back to normal in Dublin city. The shops were back open and the postal and rail services were back on schedule. But all around the country there were hotspots of trouble where rebels still fought against the Nationals.

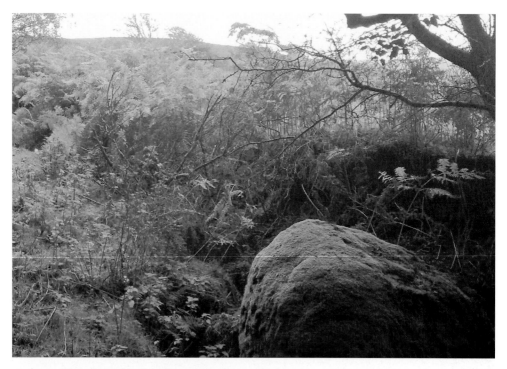

Glenasmole, the Fianna's favourite hunting ground.

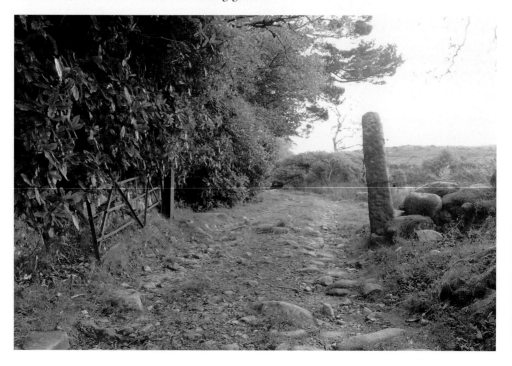

Fionn McCoole's Stone is located on the left of this pathway, behind the gate at Castlekelly.

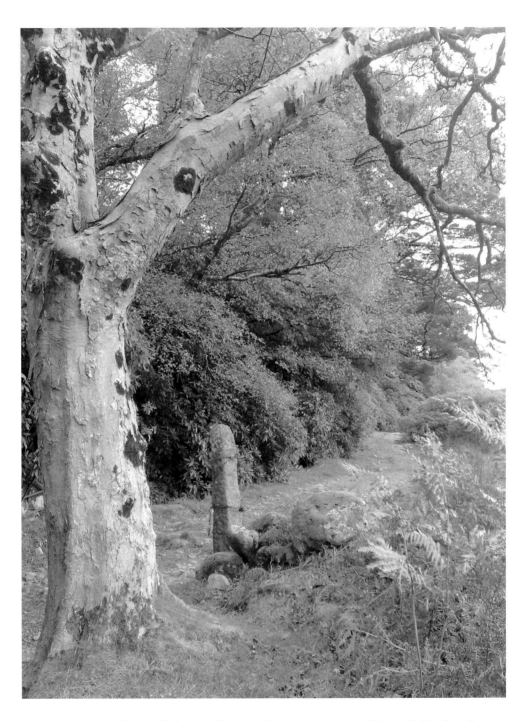

This track at Glenasmole leads to Kippure Mountain summit and Moreen's Brook to the east, believed to be the ancient site of Dá Derga's Hostel.

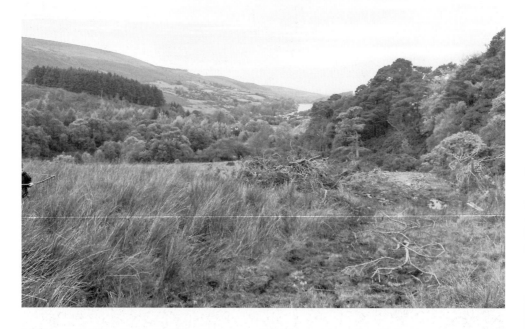

Looking down Glenasmole Valley with the reservoir lake visible in the centre.

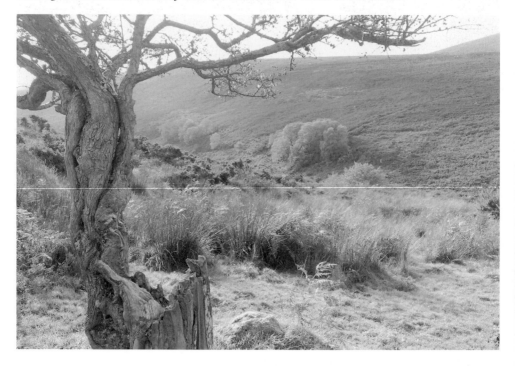

At Castlekelly bog, looking west.

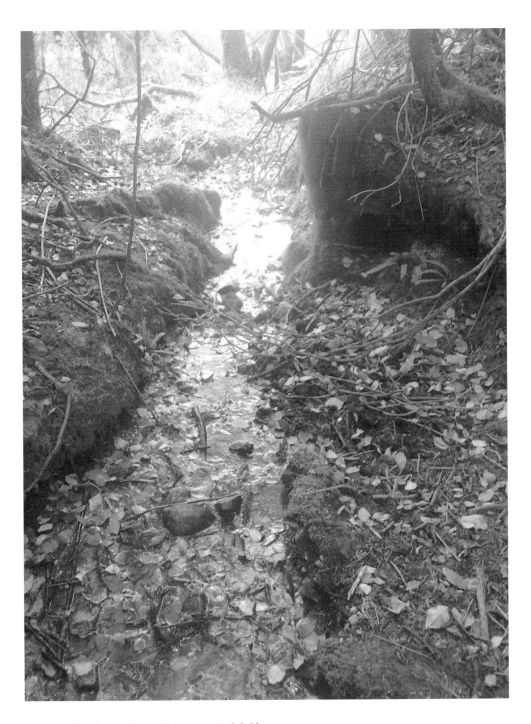

Cot Brook at Glenasmole, near Heathfield.

PLACE NAMES TRANSLATED

Aghfarrell: Farrell's field
Allagour: the cliff of the goat
Balhnascorney: the town of the gorge/ the town of the gurgling water
Ballycragh (Lower and Upper): the town of the preys
Ballycullen: Cullen's town
Ballymaice: the town of the hill
Ballyimana: the middle town
Ballymorefinn: Finn's great town
Bohernabreena: the road of the court
Brittas: the speckled lands
Castlekelly: Named after a castle that was built in the area
Corbally: the odd town
Corrageen: the little rock
Cunard: the high head
Glassamucky: the stream of the swineherd
Glassavullaun: the stream of the little summit
Killininny: the church of the daughters
Kiltalown: the church of the elm woods
Kiltipper: the church of the well
Knocklyon: Leinster hill
Lugmore: the great hollow
Montpelier, Mountseskin: the bog of the marsh
Oldbawn: the old cattle enclosure

THE HILLS IN THE AREA ARE:

Carrig:	the rock
Glassavullaun:	the stream of the little summit
Kippure:	the trunk of the yew tree; The Black hill
Montpelier:	this is a modern name, the original name is unknown
Seefin:	the seat of Fionn
Seehan:	the seat
Slievebane:	the white mountain
Slievenabawnoge:	the mountain of the lea

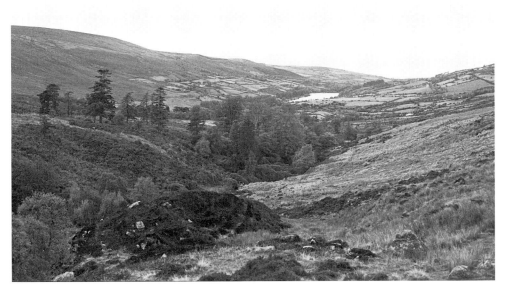

The valley looking in the direction of Dublin City. (Courtesy of South County Dublin Library)

BIBLIOGRAPHY

Aalen, F.H.A. and Whelan, Kevin, *Dublin City and County: From Prehistory to Present. Studies in Honour of J H Andrews* (Geography Publications, 1992)

Anon, *Annals of the Four Masters*

Anon, *De Shíl Chonairi Móir Liber Hymnorum of Ireland*, Vol. 2

Anon, *Lebor Gabála Érenn*

Anon, *Togail Bruidne Dá Derga* (The Destruction of Dá Derga's Hostel) translated by Whitely Stokes, DCL

Elrington Ball, Francis, *A History of the County of Dublin* (Alexander Thom & Co. Ltd, 1905)

Fanu T.P. 'The Royal Forest of Glencree' Series 5, Vol. III (1893), pp. 268-280

Handcock, William Domville, *History and Antiquities of Tallaght*, second edition (Dublin, 1899)

P.M. Haverty, *The Life and Times of Robert Emmet* (New York, 1857)

Le Fanu, T.P., 'The Royal Forest of Glencree' *Journal of the Royal Society of Antiquaries* (1893)

Little, George A., *Malachi Horan Remembers Rathfarnham and Tallaght in the Nineteenth Century* (Mercier 1943)

Madden, Richard Robert, *The life and times of Robert Emmet, with numerous notes and additions; also a memoir of Thomas Addis Emmet*

Morris, Henry, 'Where was Bruidhean Dá Derga?, *Journal of the Royal Society of Antiquaries of Ireland*, Vol. 65 (1935), pp. 297–312

Mountain, Harry, *The Celtic Encyclopedia*, Vol. 4 (Lightning Source Inc., 2011)

O'Rahilly, Thomas F., *Early Irish History and Mythology* (DIAS, 1946)

St John Joyce, Weston, *The Neighbourhood of Dublin* (M.H.Gill & Sons, 1912)

The Ossianic Society, *Transactions of the Ossianic Society*, Vol. 6

Whaley, Buck, *Buck Whaley's Memoirs* (The History Press, 2006)